DISTANCE EDUCATION SYMPOSIUM 3:

Instruction

Selected Papers Presented at
The Third Distance Education Research Symposium

The Pennsylvania State University
May 1995

Edited by

Michael F. Beaudoin

Number 12 in the series   **Research Monographs**

 American Center for the Study of Distance Education
The Pennsylvania State University
110 Rackley Building
University Park, PA 16802-3202

These papers were presented at the Third Distance Education Research Symposium, which was funded in part by AT&T.

**The American Center for the
Study of Distance Education**
The Pennsylvania State University
110 Rackley Building
University Park, PA 16802-3202

ISBN 1-877780-15-4

Table of Contents

Preface

Maintaining the Momentum

I am delighted to welcome readers to ACSDE Research Monograph No. 12, and trust that as you read the following articles, written by the leading North American researchers and thinkers about distance education, you will find much to inspire and inform you.

This monograph, Instruction, is one of a series of four, the others being Policy and Administration, Learners and Learning, and Course Design. Each monograph contains a set of articles that have been developed and edited over the past year, based on papers prepared in May 1995 for the ACSDE's Third Distance Education Research Symposium. Each monograph has been shaped and nurtured by an editor, or pair of editors, and I extend thanks to Michael F. Beaudoin, Dean and Associate Professor of Education at the University of New England, for editing Instruction.

I have given this preface the title "Maintaining the Momentum." This is because I think it is important for us to remember the precedents for this particular work, to have a sense of where it is leading us, and to appreciate that what is written here is part of an on-going, indeed, historical process.

This process began in 1986 with the founding of *The American Journal of Distance Education (AJDE)*, and the establishment soon after of the American Center for the Study of Distance Education. The basic idea of the Center and purpose of *The Journal* has been to bring people together. In the United States the study of distance education, like its practice, has been highly fragmented, with little sense of community, for example, among persons researching correspondence education, education by broadcasting, and by teleconferencing. At the American Center we have tried to provide a number of vehicles for researchers, practitioners, and students who are willing to look beyond technology, who wish to identify and research the learning, instructional design, evaluation, managerial, and policy questions in distance education.

One of the first of these vehicles was the July 1988, "First American Symposium on Research in Distance Education." This was a meeting of around forty people, most of whom had shown their interest in distance education research by having an article published in *AJDE*. They were all known to the editor of *AJDE*, but not to one another. From that meeting emerged a network of persons having a better understanding of where their piece of the distance education research agenda fitted with what was going on in the rest of the field, as well as having a common sense of what needed to be done. This was the agenda for distance education research, broken down into the themes of administration and organization, learning and learner support, course design and instruction, and theory and policy.

Thirty two papers of the First American Symposium on Research in Distance Education were published in *Contemporary Issues in American Distance Education* (Moore 1990).

Following the success of the First Symposium, ACSDE used the same format in November 1990 to organize a similar event but this time focusing on the need to articulate an agenda for distance education research that was international. The first International Symposium on Distance Education Research was held in Macuto, Venezuela, prior to the 15th World Conference of The International Council for Distance Education. Again there were around fifty participants, but this time they came from a dozen countries. Once again the focus was on the state of the research and the agenda for the years ahead, though this time the question was how colleagues could collaborate internationally, not just nationally. Papers from this Symposium were published in ACSDE Research Monograph No. 5.

The impetus towards international collaboration at the Macuto symposium had one very important consequence for the evolution of distance education as a field of study and research. This was the setting up of an electronic network, known as Distance Education Online Symposium (DEOS), one of the first in distance education. By 1996, DEOS has grown to be a network of more than 4000 participants in some sixty countries.

A Second American Symposium on Research in Distance Education was held in May 1991, bringing together in equal numbers participants from the 1988 meeting with others who had published research in *AJDE* or DEOS during the intervening years. Sixteen states were represented as well as Canada. Participants addressed the themes: What have been the results of research since the First Symposium? What are the questions for further research? A poll of participants resulted in the following "top issues":

- Interaction of learner attributes and instructional methods
- Strategies for introducing innovations in course design/delivery
- Need for and effectiveness of interaction (faculty-student, student-student)
- Faculty/administrator development (Moore et al. 1991)

The papers of this Second Symposium were published as ACSDE Research Monograph Nos. 4, 8, and 9, which are available from ACSDE.

From reading these few notes, I hope it will be apparent why I said that the 1995 Symposium should be seen in its historical context. Context will show us the progress we have made, and point to the directions ahead. Just ten years ago there was no defined field of distance education research, and it has taken just ten years to reach the level of sophistication recorded in the pages of this monograph. Context also helps us understand why we are not better than we are. Our growth has been fast, and uncontrolled, and it is not surprising that some seeds, planted hurriedly and hastily brought to blossom, have not flourished. Context, provided by the papers that record the discussions at previous symposia, should help us recognize the sturdy themes, those that have been reiterated as one set of discussants has given way to another. Since each paper cites the sources of its author's thinking, we would be foolish to pass over the opportunity of identifying the pedigree underlying any question that may now appear to be of interest. These are documents that cry out to be used as a means of providing theoretical underpinning for any new venture.

So now, I invite you to turn to Michael Beaudoin's introduction, and then the papers provided in this, the papers from ACSDE's Third American Symposium on Research in Distance Education. I expect there will be a Fourth Symposium before very long, and that perhaps you will wish to attend. Perhaps you will be able to refer to the themes identified in previous Symposia, and show how your research has advanced that agenda. If so, I will be very happy to see you.

Michael G. Moore

References

Moore M., ed. 1990. *Contemporary Issues in American Distance Education*. Oxford: Pergamon Press.

Moore, M., M. Thompson, P. Dirr, eds. 1991. Report on The Second American Symposium on Research in Distance Education. University Park, PA: The American Center for the Study of Distance Education.

1 Introduction

Michael F. Beaudoin

Being asked to moderate the presentations and discussions of research papers on instruction at the Third Invitational Research Symposium on Distance Education was an enjoyable assignment; assuming responsibility for editing these papers for inclusion in this monograph was a more challenging task; and authoring this introduction is an especially daunting charge since it requires that I extract from the work of several scholars and practitioners of distance education the most salient elements of their current research, and then suggest a research agenda derived from the observations and insights they have articulated in these papers.

A difficult task indeed, but made easier by the fact that, in addition to offering provocative ideas regarding past, present, and future research issues in distance education, these papers represent some exceptionally well crafted writing in the field. I encourage the reader to experience each piece in its entirety; they are accessible and exciting, and each makes an important contribution to the significant work we are all doing.

Relatively early in our research group's deliberations on instruction, it became apparent that the notion of interaction would be a dominant element of discussion. While not our exclusive focus, interaction emerged as a critical dimension influencing instruction in virtually every distance teaching/learning milieu we examined.

Several presentations specifically dealt with interaction and the ideas and information presented in these papers guided the overall discussion of the group. Cookson gave a progress report on an instrument to measure interaction in audioconferencing settings, adapted from previous models for face-to-face instruction. Barker gave a summary of information used in training preservice teachers to work in a distance format which would ensure interaction in telecommunicated settings. Kearsley raised questions as to the role and value of interaction and the lack of research that supports our instinctive sense that interaction is important and necessary. Saba linked the need for research on interaction in distance education to systems theory, and Tallman examined critical theory as it relates to reflective activity of instructors and empowerment of learners.

While we acknowledged Michael Moore's widely accepted typology of interaction—learner-content, learner-instructor, and learner-learner—as a framework for our exchange of views on instruction, the research presented and the group's discussions suggested that other forms of interaction have since become discernible and warrant attention and analysis. These should now augment Moore's initial construct.

Specifically, we identified at least three additional axes of interaction that the typical distant learner experiences to some degree: learner-medium; learner-institution; and learner-practice environment. Gunawardena argues that technology-mediated instruction suggests that we add learner-medium; Kascus' paper, which discusses library support as an essential ingredient to ensure quality in distance education, reminds us that the student-institution connection remains a paramount element of interactivity; and finally, I proposed that, for distant learners engaged in professional education (e.g., teachers, health providers), the interrelationships between learner-practice environment (in which they subsequently apply new knowledge and skills) is another dimension of interaction to be recognized and studied.

Underlying our discussion of interaction in various contexts was an awareness that distance educators have for too long felt compelled to simulate the interactive features typically associated with classroom-based teaching and learning, assuming that good things happen in face-to-face instruction. Finally, it now seems distance educators are moving beyond this compulsion and are defining what modes of interaction are most appropriate to their particular environment rather than attempting to replicate the best (and worse) of classroom instruction. This evolution has also led us to view the teacher/mentor more as a facilitator of the learning process in a learner-centered environment rather than a transmitter of information in a teacher-centered domain.

We also recognized and attempted to understand another subtle but significant dimension of interaction—its private and public facets. We are familiar with the more public manifestations of interaction, but the student also interacts with his or her own thoughts, values, and assumptions as they affect and influence the individual before, during, and after the learning activity in which they are engaged.

It is important to recognize that there is not usually just one mode of interaction taking place at any given moment; there is more typically a complex interplay of different types of interactivity occurring simultaneously. We should further examine causal connections between these various modes of interactivity; we might also look at what students want and/or think they need with regard to interaction and compare these with what providers creating the learning environment assume to be the most cost-effective and learner-beneficial elements of interaction.

Other key research interests around the topic of instruction were also addressed in some detail. Clark reviewed an Iowa Star Schools project and offered research implications of this model for improving instructional practices in large-scale systems. P. Gonzalez summarized a case study comparing face-to-face and on-line instruction, noting especially the public dimension of the on-line environment and its impact on the behavior of students and the role of the teacher. Jones addressed university and K-12 linkages in telecourse-mediated staff development, looking in particular at the significance of disciplines, delivery systems, populations, locations, and costs. Gunawardena and Zittle analyzed teaching and learning principles related to interaction, learner-centered instruction, social presence, cognitive strategies, collaborative learning, and constructivism as a basis for effective instructional strategies. Kascus argues that empirical studies and research data are needed to document successful outcomes of library support for distance learners. Areas for inquiry include: comparison of attitudes and performance of off-campus and on-campus students regarding library usage and measuring learning outcomes for students to become self-directed and library literate. M. Gonzalez's case study of human resources training via distance education in a Mexican company raised interesting questions regarding the interrelation of collaboration and competition as learning motivators.

These discussions generated a list of suggested research topics for further consideration. Questions relating to interaction were summarized as follows:

- Is frequency of interaction meaningful?
- Is understanding increased when interaction is present?
- Does interaction influence learner satisfaction?
- Is interaction more important for certain types of learners?
- Is there an optimum form/type of interaction in particular settings?
- What is the effect of interaction on retention?
- Are there changing patterns/levels of interaction over a course?
- What is the perception of interaction versus the use of it?
- What is the interplay between public and private interaction?
- What is the interplay between different types of simultaneous interaction?
- What interaction do students want vs. what the teacher/institution provides?

- How is cost effectiveness and learning effectiveness of interaction determined?

Several other areas of inquiry surfaced which we agreed need further consideration. These areas are summarized below.

- Best practices: Distance education practitioners are articulating so-called best practices; if they are being promulgated and adopted, should we not conduct research to verify the efficacy of these best practices?
- Qualitative, anecdotal data: Have we reached a stage in framing our research projects where we are inclined to abandon more serendipitous sources of insight that can inform our present practice and guide our future research?
- As we advance knowledge in the field through our research, are we now tending to replicate earlier research and, if so, is this useful?
- Influence of the medium: How does the medium of instruction influence the learner, the teacher, the learning group, and the dynamic involving all the principals engaged in the process?
- Impacting systems: As we move from examining small, isolated distance education projects to assessing large professional development programs that reach significant numbers of practitioners, can we identify improved quality in large systems over time?
- Research vs. reality: Should researchers be concerned about the tension that may be generated by research and the desired directions it suggests vs. the resource realities of the institution/work place and the limitations placed on decision makers?
- Parallelism: Are we spending too much of our research effort comparing what we do in distance education with "regular" education? Does it serve any useful purpose?
- How does individual and collective research influence and impact the culture of distance education?

These, then, are the ideas, issues, and areas of inquiry around the pervasive topic of instruction that distance education scholars and practitioners are currently pursuing. We invite your responses, challenges, and contributions to this work in progress as we all advance distance education toward the next millennium.

Michael F. Beaudoin

Acknowledgement

Special thanks to Judi Robie of the University of New England for her support in processing the manuscripts and facilitating communication with the authors during preparation of this monograph.

2 Strategies to Ensure Interaction in Telecommunicated Distance Learning

Bruce O. Barker

Introduction

Distance learning projects utilizing telecommunications technologies such as satellites, cable television, fiber optics, digital compression, microwave, instructional television fixed services (ITFS), etc., are being established at colleges, universities, and K-12 schools across the country. Few educational practices have caught the attention of education and policy decision makers as has the concept of distance education.

The federal and state support given to distance learning is clear indication that this approach to educational delivery is increasingly becoming an accepted method for teaching and learning, and its practice is expected to grow significantly in coming years. This growing acceptance and use of distance education demands that educational policy and decision makers address the issue of instructional effectiveness to assure that this approach to teaching/learning is correctly and optimally utilized.

Defining Telecommunicated Distance Education

In defining telecommunicated distance education, two elements are paramount—distance education is both *time* and *distance* insensitive. Hence, any definition would be incomplete without addressing both these factors. In this paper, I propose two definitions: 1) classroom-focused distance learning which emphasizes *distance* insensitivity, and 2) network-focused distance learning which emphasizes both *time* and *distance* insensitivity (Barker and Dickson 1994).

- *Classroom-Focused Distance Learning:* An accepted definition which is classroom-focused and is *distance insensitive* is the live, simultaneous transmission of a teacher's lessons from a host classroom or studio to multiple receive-site classrooms in distant locations. Two-way live communication in real time, whether audio or video between the teacher and students, permits the instruction to be interactive. This model implies that instruction is oriented more toward small groups or clusters of students at different sites than to an individual student. Under ideal conditions, students at any one site are not only provided direct contact with their instructor but are also able to communicate directly with students at other remote sites during the instructional process (Barker, Frisbie, and Patrick 1995).

- *Network-Focused Distance Learning:* The classroom-focused definition, though accurate in regard to the issue of *distance insensitivity* does not allow for flexibility in regard to *time.* This is true for both instructor and students. Today's digital revolution and the exponential growth of the Internet have given rise to a plethora of informational and educational wonders available through computer networks. While most of the information on the Internet remains text-based, the release of Internet "browsers" such as the National Center for Supercomputing Applications' (NCSA) Mosaic™ in early 1994 and the commercial release of Netscape™ in late 1994 have made available thousands of materials on the Internet which combine text, audio, graphics, and short video clips. All this information can be downloaded and viewed on one's personal computer at one's own time and leisure. The services of the Internet permit individuals to gather information, keep current on virtually any topic of interest, and communicate with others across the country or around the world at their own time convenience. The potential for learning via the Internet is incomprehensible. In fact, it is plausible that network-focused distance learning which is both *time* and *distance insensitive*—coupled with the exponential growth of the Internet—will one day eclipse the practice of classroom-focused distance learning.

The Teacher's Role in Successful Distance Education Programs

The bulk of attention given telecommunicated distance education today is classroom-focused. Although the Internet and the World Wide Web—with their accompanying bulletin boards, e-mail services, and ubiquitous databases of text, images, sound, and motion files—are continually growing in number, the thought of a "master" instructor speaking to and interacting with students in remote locations simultaneously is the present model for most distance learning programs.

Success of classroom-focused distance learning programs is ultimately dependent upon the manner and quality of instruction delivered. From the U.S. Office of Technology Assessment's landmark study, *Linking for Learning: A New Course for Education,* the following are among findings noted as successful practices of ongoing classroom-focused distance education programs (U.S. Congress 1989, pp. 87–88):

- *The key to success in distance learning is the teacher.* If the teacher on the system is good, the technology itself can become almost transparent. Conversely, no technology can overcome poor teaching; poor teaching is actually exacerbated in distance education applications. But when skilled teachers are involved, enthusiasm, expertise, and creative use of the media can enrich students beyond the four walls of their home classroom. Outstanding teachers can also serve as "electronic mentors" to other teachers.

- *Teachers using distance learning have had to find new ways to structure student-teacher interaction.* Old styles of teaching may not be appropriate or effective. The inherent limitations in distance learning technologies can be catalysts for instructional design and teaching techniques that enhance the learning process.

- *Teachers must be trained if they are to use distance learning technologies effectively.* Training opportunities, however, remain limited. Few preservice and inservice programs focus on how to incorporate technology into instruction, create new opportunities for interactivity, or develop materials and use the media most effectively.

Distance education instructors of necessity must be master teachers. They must understand and model principles from the literature on effective teaching, and know how to best use technology to convey their teaching. Teachers must possess a "presence" that capitalizes on the use of the television as a teaching medium. In this respect, much can be learned from broadcast journalism— that is, noting how TV anchors look directly into the camera, are precise and articulate in their selection of words, and support their presentations with a high level of visual content (Barker and Dickson 1994).

Distance teaching pedagogy also requires "forced" interaction between teacher and students, a slower pace of instruction, and clear logical presentations. The teacher needs to ask a lot of questions to ascertain if students understand and to keep them actively involved in the instructional process.

"Forced" Interaction in Telecommunicated Distance Learning

The responsibility for effective interaction in telecommunicated distance learning programs is the direct responsibility of the instructor (Winn 1990). In most instances, the instructor must plan for and employ purposeful strategies to initiate and promote interaction. Otherwise, distance students are likely to gravitate to a passive role during the instructional process. Some techniques to help ensure that high levels of teacher-student and student-to-student interaction occur in the distance learning exchange include (Oliver 1994, pp. 184–185):

- Pre-determine a block of time for interaction and advise students in advance when interaction is anticipated. Provide an advance organizer to enable students to prepare for the interactive segment.

- Integrate on-air interaction with on-site activities or assignments prepared in advance of interaction.

- Designate specific students or sites to call in with responses, comments, or questions. An unstructured invitation to call in will not ensure a response.

- Motivate interaction with structured silence. Avoid "filling in time" with potentially distracting activities while waiting for calls.

- Vary the timing of interactive segments: prior to, during, and following information presentation. Continued deferral of interaction until after information presentation may reinforce passive viewing.

- Encourage student-to-student interaction and ensure opportunities for social affiliation. Ask a host-site student or a student from a different site to respond to a caller. Questions do not always have to be answered by the instructor.

- Establish greeting protocols to facilitate social affiliation.

Additional considerations for promoting high levels of interaction include (Baker 1994; Barker and Goodwin 1992; Ostendorf 1989):

- *Initiate interaction within the first twenty minutes of a telecast.* If immediate interaction does not occur, distance students are likely to remain passive rather than active learners.

- *"Prime" participants for interaction.* Distance students should be reminded ahead of time that an interactive segment is forthcoming and that their opinions will be solicited.

- *Involve participants in discussion.* Assign questions to remote site students prior to the telecast. This helps assure that learners will come prepared for interaction. Furthermore, efforts should be made to involve all learners in class activities. Calling students by name to participate in class discussions will personalize lessons as well as notify students that they are each responsible to participate as active learners. Directed questions to a specific student(s) can be an effective approach in gaining more student participation. The instructor might also maintain a log, by student name, of who is participating and who is not. This can be used as a record to help remind the teacher to call upon noncontributing members in the class or to more equitably distribute teacher-student interactions.

- *Ask "low" order and "high" order questions.* Questions to learners should be preplanned and range from low order (recall or knowledge) to higher order (synthesis, analysis, problem solving). The teacher needs to ask a lot of questions to "force" interaction with students. After posing a question, the teacher should allow sufficient "wait time" for students to process information before answering.

- *Clear teacher articulation.* The instructor must articulate clearly and distinctly. Verbal instructions from the teacher must be precise and explicit. Too much teacher-talk, especially if the teacher is rambling, can cause confusion. Also, a voice that portrays enthusiasm, variety in tone, and diversity in pace will do much to maintain student interest and cause students to want to be active participants in the learning process.

- *Use variety to involve students.* Watching the TV screen for a long period of time without interaction or involvement from students can be deadly. Brief teacher lectures (no more than twenty minutes) interspersed with questions works well. Other student involvement activities might include small-group work, dyad discussions, cooperative learning tasks, student presentations, discussions between students at two or more different sites, polling of students among all sites to seek their opinion, etc.

- *Appropriate use of humor.* Introducing humor to the class through examples and by poking fun at the technology, class events, or oneself add a "spark" to the class which maintains the interest and involvement of students. Participating in friendly banter with students prior to class, while taking roll, during break, or while otherwise interacting over the telecommunications systems also helps personalize social exchanges between instructor and students.

Distance Learner Responsibilities to Promote Interaction

While the responsibility to ensure high levels of teacher-student and student-student interaction in telecommunicated distance learning rests with the instructor, a portion of that responsibility must be delegated to the distant students if they are to be more than passive learners. For most students, learning at a distance is a new experience, and one which they will need to adapt to. Advice directed to remote site students to help them take greater responsibility for their own success include (Baker 1994):

- *Distance students must be assertive.* This means: if you have a question during class, speak up. At first, it may seem like you are forcing yourself on the instructor or that you are being rude because you feel like you are interrupting. Courteously say, "I have a question" or "May I make a comment?"

- *Sit near the microphone and the TV monitor at your site for two reasons:* 1) so you can see and hear the instructor, and 2) so the instructor can see and hear you when you interact.

- *Get to know other students at your site.* Much of the learning that occurs in class is "informal learning" between you and your classmates.

- *Overcome home TV viewing habits.* Watching television at home is a VERY different activity than watching and participating in a TV class. Many people at home watch TV while they are doing something else (e.g., eating, sewing, paying bills, reading, etc.) or they may watch TV to "unwind" or relax. Participation in an interactive TV class requires that you interact. Students must stay focused, ask questions (talk to the TV teacher and classmates), share ideas, etc. Students must be active, not passive learners.

- *Contact TV instructor after class.* Contact the instructor by telephone during his/her office hours if you have questions that cannot be answered during the interactive class time.

Conclusion

Telecommunicated distance learning technologies, specifically TV instruction, have a relatively short history beginning in the late 1950s and early 1960s with one-way passive viewing of educational broadcast television. Since that early beginning, we have seen the implementation of ITFS, cable television, and microwave integrated with audio talk-back as mediums for distance learning. In the mid-1980s we saw the advent of interactive satellite which also permits one-way video, two-way audio interaction. In the late 1980s and early

1990s, however, we have witnessed increased use of two-way video and two-way audio either over fiber optic connections or compressed television. Each iteration of televised instruction has seen an increased capability of interaction between the TV instructor and remote site students. Clearly, the focus in each level of technology advancement has been for better and higher levels of interaction.

What are the implications for further research on the perceived value of student interaction in telecommunicated distance learning? In addition to strategies mentioned in this paper, it would seem that a careful analysis of effective teaching practices in traditional classrooms would suggest other specific strategies which are also applicable to distance learning environments. Can too much emphasis be placed on getting students to actively participate in the learning process? If so, where is the proper balance? Furthermore, is some instructional content more conducive—and perhaps more important—for interaction than is other content? What role do CD-ROMs, the Internet, e-mail, print, facsimile machines, or other media have in promoting interaction? What are the relationships between interaction in distance learning and student achievement? These questions suggest only a few of potentially many topics for further data gathering and research on the role of student interaction in distance learning.

The responsibility rests with distance educators to design and deliver instruction which integrate strategies for interaction between themselves and their students in order to promote increased learning. Furthermore, distance students must accept greater responsibility for their own learning by becoming active participants in the instructional process.

References

Baker, M. H. 1994. Distance teaching with interactive television: Strategies that promote interaction with remote-site students. Unpublished doctoral dissertation. Iowa City, IA: University of Iowa.

Barker, B. O., and M. W. Dickson. 1994. Aspects of successful practice for working with college faculty in distance education programs. *Education at a Distance* 8(2):6–10.

Barker, B. O., A. Frisbie, and K. Patrick. 1995. Broadening the definition of distance education in light of the new telecommunications technologies. In *Video-based Telecommunications in Distance Education,* Readings in Distance Education Number 4, eds. M. Moore and M. Koble, 1–10. University Park, PA: The American Center for the Study of Distance Education, The Pennsylvania State University.

Barker, B. O., and R. D. Goodwin. 1992. Audiographics: Linking remote classrooms. *The Computing Teacher* 19(7):11–15.

Oliver, E. L. 1994. Video tools for distance education. In *Distance Education: Strategies and Tools,* ed. B. Willis, 165–197. Englewood Cliffs, NJ: Educational Technology Publications.

Ostendorf, V. A. 1989. *Teaching Through Interactive Television.* Littleton, CO: Virginia A. Ostendorf, Inc.

U.S. Congress, Office of Technology Assessment. 1989. *Linking for learning: A new course for education* (OTA-SET-430). Washington, DC: U.S. Government Printing Office.

Winn, B. 1990. Media and instructional methods. In *Education at a Distance: From Issues to Practice,* eds. D. R. Garrison and D. Shale, 53–66. Malabar, FL: Robert E. Krieger Publishing.

<table>
<tr><td>3</td><td>The IDEA: An Iowa Approach to Improving Instructional Quality

Tom Clark</td></tr>
</table>

3

The IDEA: An Iowa Approach to Improving Instructional Quality

Tom Clark

Project Overview

The Iowa Communications Network (ICN), is an audio, video, and data fiber optic network currently connecting over 130 two-way full-motion (DS-3) video classrooms across the state. The comprehensive statewide coverage of the system, public rather than private ownership of the network, and full-motion video capabilities make the network unique among state-level telecommunications systems in the United States.

Construction began on the network in 1991, and by December 1994 the ICN had already connected 99 counties with 3,000 miles of fiber, linking 124 school and college classrooms equipped for video-based distance learning in Parts One and Two of the project (Iowa Public Television 1994). Construction of the third part of the ICN is planned to begin in 1995, with various scenarios connecting up to 500 schools, libraries, and area education agencies to the network.

The National Guard, which houses the central video switcher for the statewide network in its STARC Armory, is building its own armory network interconnected with the ICN. Some state agencies and hospitals have also built ICN rooms linked to the network. State government and public postsecondary educational institutions have already moved video, voice, and data services previously purchased from the private sector onto the Network (Iowa Public Television 1994).

Project Background. On September 24, 1992, a two-year $8 million grant was awarded to the Iowa Distance Education Alliance (IDEA) under the auspices of the Iowa Public Broadcasting Board and the Iowa Department of Education, through the United States Department of Education's Star Schools Program. Through this grant, the Alliance was to demonstrate the use of the Iowa Communication Network's (ICN) fiber optic technology for K-12–related instruction and training (IDEA 1992).

IDEA Partnership. The IDEA partnership included representatives from Iowa Public Television, the Iowa Department of Education, the state's three public universities, area education agencies (AEAs) and community colleges in each of the state's fifteen merged areas, independent colleges and universities, and local school districts, with support from teacher, administrator, and school board professional associations (IDEA 1992).

The authors of the original grant proposal hoped that the IDEA would

> ...be a model for other states and regions that plan the large scale implementation of a distance education system that is based on the concept of local control of courses offered using live two-way interactive telecommunications. (Simonson, Sweeney, and Kemis 1993, 28)

Project Components. The IDEA Project had four components: Project Management, the Communication and Resources Clearinghouse, Regional Partnerships, and the Teacher Education Alliance (TEA). Project Management staff coordinated communication among components, and worked with the Regional Partnerships and the TEA to ensure that project goals were met. The Clearinghouse was established to provide access to project-related information for participants and coordinate access to other networks. An Iowa Database housed on a World Wide Web server was created for this purpose, and Internet training was built into project planning.

Community colleges and AEAs in each merged area of the state formed Regional Partnerships and designated a regional coordinator (Simonson, Sweeney, and Kemis 1993). Each regional partnership collaborated with the TEA and Project Management to inform Iowans about the ICN, coordinate K-12 activities, and provide teacher training in distance education and curriculum development in its merged area (Sorensen and Sweeney 1994).

Faculty from the three public universities in Iowa coordinated the TEA, working closely with independent college faculty and the area education agencies. The TEA coordinated K-12 teacher preservice and inservice components of the Project and developed a plan for research and evaluation of the project (Simonson, Sweeney, and Kemis 1993, 23).

In summarizing their key findings, the authors of the Final Evaluation Report concluded that:

All of the objectives and activities outlined in the IDEA proposal were accomplished during the two years of the project, and the momentum begun with the project is continuing. Cooperation and collaboration among educational organizations in Iowa improved. Innovative instructional activities are occurring over the ICN. Students and teachers who used the system view it positively. (Sorensen and Sweeney 1994, i)

External Recognition of the Project. Besides positive reviews from external evaluators, the IDEA received several national awards in 1994-1995 for the Iowa Star Schools project. Project documents and videos were distributed to regional coordinators and participating institutions throughout Iowa and were made available at cost to other interested parties within Iowa and nationally.

Project Findings

Evaluation Findings. The Iowa Star Schools project focused on accomplishing six major goals, which in their abbreviated format were:

1. coordinating use of the ICN,
2. informing Iowans about the ICN,
3. preparing teachers to use the ICN,
4. connecting schools to the ICN,
5. improving instruction in five content areas through use of the ICN, and
6. documenting the effectiveness of project use of the ICN. (Sorensen and Sweeney 1994, i)

Iowa Approach. The Iowa Approach called for cooperation and collaboration among project partners to use the state's unique interactive technologies in a flexible and cost-effective manner to accomplish project goals of improving K-12 education. Existing institutions and relationships were utilized, rather than creating new organizational infrastructures less likely to continue innovations after the project's end. Inclusiveness and equal partnership were central tenets of the IDEA, which embodied this approach.

The major focus in the present paper is on the modeling and dissemination of effective instructional practices, therefore, the emphasis in this review will be on goals three and six. Other goals will be dealt with only to the extent that they are relevant to effective instructional practice.

Preparing Teachers to use the ICN

Teacher Education Alliance. Goal three, in its long form, stated "Iowa educators will be prepared and supported so they can effectively teach students at a distance" (Sorensen and Sweeney 1994, 26). Under this goal, the Teacher Education Alliance (TEA) provided teacher inservice training related both to distance learning and curriculum reform, and facilitated the integration of distance learning components into preservice teacher education programs at colleges and universities throughout the state. The TEA attempted to impart an Iowa philosophy or idea to participating teachers. This philosophy called for interactive, student-centered teaching, and for local control of the curriculum, with sharing of instructional resources and activities via a statewide network. (Simonson 1993).

Inservice Workshops. About 900 Iowa educators, mostly K-12 teachers but including some community college instructors and area education agency personnel, attended one of the thirty-five three-day hands-on workshops conducted throughout the state during the project. Dr. Robert Hardman of the University of Northern Iowa (UNI) acted as Teacher Inservice Coordinator, while Dr. Sharon Smaldino of UNI and Dr. Ann Thompson of Iowa State University acted as Teacher Preservice Co-Coordinators.

The primary purpose of each workshop was to introduce educators to the use of interactive television for distance education. Over the long term, it was intended that workshop participants would act as "mentors" who can assist other educators in the use of interactive television in their institution, local district, and region.

Pre-assessment instruments were completed by 340 of the 1992-1993 workshop participants, and post-assessment instruments by 295 participants. Paired t-tests showed significant differences on each item, indicating that participants felt they had become more knowledgeable about every aspect of the workshop content. The content included:

- The unique characteristics of interactive television, and a rationale for its use.
- Components of an interactive television system, and its operation.
- Resources needed to use the system.
- Strategies for teaching over interactive television.
- Strategies for evaluating interactive television instruction.
- Research findings and critical issues related to the use of interactive television (Hardman 1993; Sorensen and Sweeney 1994, 271–290).

For a substantial part of the time in most workshops, participants were divided between two ICN classrooms. Attendees prepared five-minute lessons and presented them over the system to the participants acting as remote students at the other site. Feedback between participants was highly encouraged. Overall evaluations of the interactive workshops by the 302 respondents were highly positive, with ratings averaging more than 4.5 on a scale from 1 to 5, where 5 denoted "excellent" (Sorensen and Sweeney 1994). Asked to list the components of the workshop most useful to them, the large majority of responding participants cited actual use of the equipment (Sorensen and Sweeney 1994).

Curriculum Institutes. A total of 555 K-12 educators, including representatives from each of Iowa's 99 counties attended curriculum reform institutes in five targeted content areas (mathematics, science, foreign language, literacy, and vocational education). During the first year, the institutes were held at university sites. The second year, the general curriculum sessions were conducted over the ICN at twenty-two ICN sites around the state. While content area sessions were held in various formats, participants rated the institutes overall as 'above average' to 'excellent' both years; however, ratings were lower in the second year (Sorensen and Sweeney 1994). ICN logistical problems and a preference for direct interaction with the teacher may have been factors in the less favorable second year ratings. The institutes with fewer participants were rated higher both years.

Participant Follow-up. In September 1994, a follow-up survey was administered to participants in the curriculum institutes and inservice interactive workshops. Of the 710 teachers, surveyed, 325 replied (46%). The demographics of respondents were similar to those of all participants. About one in five had used the ICN for instructional activities by the time of the survey. When asked to list issues that needed to be addressed for successful teaching over the ICN, 107 participants cited access to an ICN site or equity in site selection as an important issue, fifty-four mentioned teacher preparation, and fifty-three cited ICN training. Asked to cite one issue of greatest concern, ninety-seven chose access and equity, and thirty-two cited local costs. Many of these teachers considered planning time, release time, and pay for ICN teaching as issues that needed to be addressed (Sorensen and Sweeney 1994).

Preservice Activities. In addition to inservice activities, preservice activities were undertaken by the TEA for the purpose of encouraging the integration of distance education into teacher education curricula. An Interactive Television Preservice Resource Guidebook was developed and distributed to teacher education programs, as was a monograph of curriculum reform papers. A series of conference presentations, colloquia, and workshops were offered for Iowa teacher educators throughout the project. In Fall 1994, the department chairs of twenty-two of the twenty-eight independent college and university teachers responded to a telephone follow-up survey. Faculty training, access to an ICN room, and financial resources were most frequently mentioned by the department chairs surveyed as issues related to the integration of distance education into the curricula of responding teacher education programs (Sorensen and Sweeney 1994).

Integration into Preservice Education. Since four-year college and university faculty training was not part of the Star Schools project, due to the nature of the grant legislation, the long-term impact of the project on these independent colleges may be expected to be limited. However, some of the independents, such as Drake University, Buena Vista College, and Iowa Wesleyan University, participated actively in the project and are likely to integrate distance education into their teacher education curricula. Recognizing the conservative nature of most Iowa teacher education programs, Herring et al. (1993) presented a preservice model mainly intended for infusion of distance learning knowledge and techniques into existing courses within teacher education preservice programs, rather than for the development of new courses centering on distance learning.

Project Evaluation

Goal six was stated fully as "A program of research and evaluation will be established to document the impact and effectiveness of the live, interactive, two-way interactive concept of distance education practiced in Iowa" (Sorensen and Sweeney 1994, 27).

A Research and Evaluation Advisory Panel was established. Data were collected from all project partners throughout the project and databases were established. Software include SPSS and Alpha Four. Results from data analyses were provided to Project Management and appropriate project partners throughout the project. A variety of instruments were developed by the evaluation team for qualitative and quantitative data collection throughout the project. During each year of the project, three external evaluators reviewed the project by examining internal evaluation data, meeting with project partners, touring facilities, and observing ICN activities. Conclusions were positive (Sorensen and Sweeney 1994). Project surveys, interviews, focus groups, and monitoring of ICN programming were used to provide a comprehensive picture of participants and their project-related activities. The evaluation plan of the project drew substantially upon the previous work of the Eastern Iowa Community College District (EICCD) in the development of its Televised Interactive Network (Kabat and Friedel 1990). The EICCD handbook was also used as a model for program development in the project's interactive workshops.

Under goal six, a number of activities were also undertaken to develop and disseminate knowledge about interactive distance learning and the Iowa Star Schools project to both participants and external audiences. The TEA published a monthly newsletter, prepared a monograph on distance education published by the Association for Educational Communications and Technology (Schlosser and Anderson 1994), funded sixteen research projects subsequently published in a compilation (Sorensen et al. 1995), prepared a series of eight single concept videos for distribution to preservice teacher education programs, assembled a library of distance education documents, and published articles in professional journals. An additional project overview video was developed for statewide and national distribution.

Project Research Related to Effective Instructional Practices

In addition to the evaluation activities and instruments administered by project staff as part of the evaluation plan, the TEA funded mini-grants for sixteen small research projects conducted by individuals and groups at educational institutions participating in the Alliance. The results of these research projects were subsequently reported in the Encyclopedia of Distance Education Research (Sorensen et al. 1995). The TEA also funded a comprehensive review of the distance education research literature related to the project (Schlosser and Anderson 1994), and a preservice guidebook featuring a research-based curriculum infusion model (Herring et al. 1993).

These small projects differed substantially in the rigor of their research approaches. Most of the research conducted was directly or peripherally related to the modeling and dissemination of effective instructional practices. A summary of findings from the most relevant small project reports follows. These research articles can be grouped into four broad categories: adoption of innovation, general teacher attitudes, effective instructional practices, and student perceptions.

Adoption of Innovation. Abou-Dagga and Herring (1995) surveyed participants in the sixteen interactive television workshops and inservice curriculum institutes conducted in 1993. Of the 475 teachers and administrators surveyed, 280 (59%) responded; 210 respondents were teachers. Participants attended for varying reasons, but those attending due to personal interest held more favorable attitudes toward the use of distance education. Teachers attending both inservice institutes and workshops were more knowledgeable and willing to use interactive television for teaching. The authors concluded that inservice coordinators "should offer a variety of experiences and viewpoints to address the beliefs and knowledge levels of participants."

Merkley, Bozik, and Oakland (1995) administered the 35-item Stages of Concern Questionnaire (SoCQ) to thirty K-12 teachers chosen by their regional coordinators to participate in a Fall 1993 Literacy Curriculum Institute. Four instructors who had high scores on two indicators of stages of concern were recruited to serve as study group members. They submitted biweekly teaching logs on their distance-education–related activities for the next seven months. Two of the four were individually interviewed at the end of this period about their distance-education–related activities and the effect of support services in their implementation of distance education. Evidence gathered suggested that teachers needed more support in assuming ownership of interactive television teaching.

Fagan (1995) mailed a descriptive survey to the seventy-five K-12 teachers who had participated in a mathematics curriculum institute during the 1992-1993 academic year. Forty-four teachers (59%) responded. Almost all were aware of distance education in this retrospective survey, but half had personal negative concerns about interactive television teaching. Male respondents, K-4 teachers, and those attending the institute, but not an interactive teaching workshop, were more likely to have personal negative concerns. About one in four had intense task-related or management concerns about using the system. The author suggested that interaction should be facilitated between teachers with positive and negative concern and that support was needed for those with management concerns. These three research projects related to adoption of innovation indicated that teachers had basic awareness of distance education but needed support and interaction with their peers to become successful adopters of the technology.

Teacher Attitudes. Miller (1995) sent a questionnaire with sections on attitudes toward ICN, perceived obstacles to ICN use, priorities for collaboration/course offerings, and respondent demographics to a random sample of 140 Iowa secondary agricultural education teachers drawn from the total population. Of those surveyed, 102 (73%) responded. About two in three respondents indicated they were undecided about their potential use of the ICN to teach agriculture, while nearly one-third showed positive attitudes toward system use. School and class scheduling problems were cited as the most significant obstacles by instructors, on average. Theoretical courses were most often mentioned as courses instructors would be willing to teach over the system, while applied courses were most often mentioned as unsuitable for ICN. The author recommended that laboratory and supervised agricultural experience demonstration programs be developed. He suggested that activities to increase instructor awareness of the ICN be emphasized despite the remoteness of ICN sites for most instructors. He also suggested that collaborative efforts be undertaken in content areas, such as agricultural economics, to serve schools without agriculture instructors.

Effective Instructional Practices. Baker (1995) combined naturalistic study of five community college teachers and surveys of their students to examine the interactive teaching strategies, tactics, and behaviors used by experienced distance instructors in different disciplines. She observed, interviewed, and videotaped the teachers at the beginning, middle, and end of their course; surveyed their students (N=95) at the same junctures; conducted two focus group sessions with remote students from both classes; and then undertook a data analysis process leading to the grouping of most teaching behaviors into seven broad categories.

Nonverbal immediacy behaviors (perceived warmth and closeness), verbalization, personalization of the class experience, and feedback methods were quite similar among these instructors, while they differed widely in their management of technology and student participation and use of active learning strategies. While nearly nine in ten students surveyed preferred teaching styles that allowed interaction between student and teacher, seven in ten felt as comfortable participating as in traditional classes. Over half also indicated a need for support of their ideas to feel comfortable participating.

Baker felt that the faculty studied showed control over three out-of-class variables that merited attention: they demonstrated belief in the value of verbal participation, involved remote site students to control the effects of remote-site-student camaraderie, or the lack thereof, and exhibited a willingness to be contacted outside of class. She felt that all three of these behaviors probably increased in-class interaction. The author recommended eye contact with and monitoring of remote-site students, and the use of alternatives to nonverbal clues, as ways for instructors to promote their comfortable interactive participation in distance courses.

Student Perceptions. Sorensen (1995) studied college student attitudes toward ICN instruction, especially student satisfaction, by surveying learners enrolled in eighteen community college courses offered over the ICN during the 1994 summer session. Two-hundred and ten of 364 students (64%) responded. More than three of every four students gave positive responses on nineteen of the twenty-five survey items about the course, including items rating interaction with the teacher and feelings of inclusion in the class. More than one in four cited distractions, feelings that other sites were not included or inhibitions about participating. Remote-site students indicated less satisfaction in several areas than origination-site students.

Survey items were grouped into course constructs. All constructs were rated positively overall on the four-point Likert (where 1=strongly agree and 4=strongly disagree) with students agreeing about overall satisfaction (Mn=3.23), technical quality (Mn=3.21), instructional quality/instructor interaction (Mn=3.17), and course membership/peer interaction (Mn=3.12), but not agreeing as strongly about the adequacy of course management (Mn=2.93). Males rated membership and instructional quality significantly more positively than females, while those over twenty-five years of age rated membership more highly than younger students.

Using the construct of overall satisfaction as the dependent variable, Sorensen found that perceptions of instructional quality, membership, and technical quality only accounted for 53 percent of the variance in stepwise regression. The primary predictor of satisfaction appeared to be perceived quality of instruction, especially for remote site students, who on average felt less need for class membership. Remote site students rated instructional quality significantly lower and were less satisfied with the course. This finding was interesting in that an IDEA evaluation survey of 177 K-12 students in sixteen ICN courses found that remote students were more satisfied with their learning experiences (Sorensen and Sweeney 1994). In response to open ended questions about things they liked about taking interactive television classes, students most often cited interaction with students at other sites, the new learning experience, and lack of travel. They were most likely to cite technical and logistical problems when asked to make suggestions for improvement.

The Baker and Sorensen studies appeared to support the interactive workshop guidelines for effective teaching, which had been based on generally accepted good instructional practices drawn from largely anecdotal literature on effective distance teaching practice. Baker's study provided qualitative support for these accepted practices, while pointing out problems with remote site interaction. Sorensen's study identified similar difficulties related to overall satisfaction based on student perceptions of interactive television.

Related Research and Projects

Moore and Thompson (1990) noted that researchers had rarely focused on the effectiveness of distance teaching for in-service K-12 teacher training. The training of college and university teachers for participation in distance teaching, a related topic, has occurred at the institutional, consortia, and state system levels, but is also the topic of limited research related to training effectiveness.

Other Star Schools Projects. Congress created the Star Schools Program in 1988 to develop multi-state, multi-institution, elementary to secondary school distance education, authorizing an expenditure of $100 million over a five-year period (Brown and Brown 1994). One of the largest examples of Star Schools in-service K-12 teacher training was the Midlands Consortium, headquartered at Oklahoma State University in Stillwater, Oklahoma. The grant totaled $9.6 million in FY 1988-89, and twenty-eight satellite-delivered staff development programs were offered to more than 10,000 teachers (OERI January 1993).

Finding a Larger Context. The U.S. Congress mandated a final evaluation of the Star Schools Program in its 1991 reauthorization. In a paper based on the first part of this mandated report, the evaluators noted the positive self-reports of changes in teacher attitude and behavior in TEAMS (Tele-communications Education Advances in Mathematics and Science), and MCET (Massachusetts Corporation for Educational Telecommunications), two Star Schools projects providing supplemental instruction to assist teachers with instructional strategies, materials, and technology use. MCET provided a variety of technologies for possible teacher use, finding that the most flexible technologies—computers, telephone, and television—were used more heavily than fixed-time satellite broadcasts, even though satellite instruction was a major focus of the project.

Tushnet (1995) felt that video technologies had been used in Star Schools projects mainly to replicate existing classroom teaching methods and that Star

Schools projects often saw declining enrollment and received little feedback from participants in satellite-videoconference-delivered traditional inservice programs. She viewed efforts to deliver teacher inservice and preservice content via computer and multimedia methods positively. Training for distance teaching and modeling of effective distance teaching behaviors did not play a large role in most Star Schools projects, according to Tushnet (1995). She noted that most studio teacher training for distance teaching was limited and involved only a few individuals.

The program evaluators in the mandated study concluded that supplemental instruction and activities aimed at achieving educational reform—a major focus in later projects, including the Iowa project—required "...collaboration with teachers so they become comfortable with the technology, understand the cognitive and pedagogical demands of the reform, and are able to use the curriculum and instructional methods to advance student learning" (Tushnet et al. 1994, 39). The program evaluators suggested that Congress consider three different future programmatic approaches for the three different goals apparent in the Star Schools Programs: improving access to educational opportunities, contributing to education reform, and demonstrating applications of emerging technologies (Tushnet et al. 1994).

Future Research Directions

The small research projects funded through the TEA, and the IDEA's evaluation research studies, suggested several areas of additional research for the improvement of instructional quality.

Learner Perceptions. The parallelism of live distance teaching, which is perhaps most complete when full-motion two-way video is used, allows students to constantly compare the quality of their learning experience with that of on-campus origination site students and students at other remote sites. Logistical and technical problems and ineffective use of interactive teaching methods may lower their perceptions of instructional quality and their satisfaction with the course. Feelings of inequitable access may affect perception as well. In statewide courses, students may expect classes to be delivered to far more sites than teachers are willing to teach to and feel discriminated against when they must drive to a regional site. The roles played by different factors in off-campus learner perceptions of satisfaction in two-way video teaching need more study.

Best Practices. A number of approaches have been taken by previous researchers in trying to provide evidence for the best instructional practices for teaching via two-way video. Qualitative studies utilizing interaction analysis, such as the one by Baker (1995) reported herein, are important in developing models. The interactive workshop model developed for the IDEA, and the philosophy of teaching it propounded, was based on practices and philosophies recommended in the literature; it was not truly research-based. Student, teacher, and expert perceptions of best practices need further study in developing a better grounding in research for best instructional practices.

Retrospective Study. There is a strong need to perform follow-up studies over time, to see if goals such as preparing and supporting ICN teachers, improving instruction, and documenting the impact and effectiveness of instruction will continue in the absence of Star Schools funding. The Iowa Star Schools project can also be seen as the beginning of a long-term research and development demonstration project on applications of emerging technologies, along the lines suggested by the program evaluators (Tushnet et al. 1994).

Implications for University Teaching

Project Activities. Project activities undertaken by the IDEA have important implications for efforts by college and university systems, in terms of their efforts to improve instructional quality through the modeling and dissemination of effective instructional practices. Relevant contributions of the IDEA's Iowa Star Schools project include: The IDEA, and its approach to collaboration and consortia; the Iowa philosophy of interactive teaching, the interactive workshop and curriculum institute models; IDEA project evaluation measures related to the adoption of innovation and effective instructional practices, as well as IDEA-funded research projects in these same areas.

Interactive Workshops. Many Iowa colleges and universities have offered interactive workshops for their own faculty and staff since the inception of the Star Schools project, building on the materials and format originally used by the TEA to train K-12 educators statewide. At Iowa State, faculty training workshops have been shortened and a collegial "hands on" approach taken, with one-on-one follow-up with instructional designers encouraged. Almost all instructors have attended a workshop before teaching on the system. Workshop facilitators at Iowa State encourage teachers to teach in their own styles, adding interactive techniques and the use of media capabilities of ICN classrooms to the degree to which they are comfortable.

Some peer networks were developed in the Star Schools project through the TEA's curriculum institutes and interactive workshops, as participants continued to communicate and to "mentor" other teachers in their schools. At Iowa State University, peer networking has been encouraged through the ICN teaching workshops and the development of a distance education interest group, which meets monthly at locations in different academic and support units. Faculty, staff, and students appear to feel comfortable sharing their experiences in this informal setting. While peer networks have grown among Iowa community colleges in areas such as Tech Prep, they are not as evident among Iowa universities.

The IDEA. The IDEA, created to improve elementary and secondary education, and the Iowa Approach it followed, can serve as a model for collaboration and cooperation among K-12 and postsecondary education-related institutions as they strive to improve the quality of instruction. By adding appropriate functions to existing entities, the IDEA, coordinating with the legislature and state agencies, appears to have been successful, at least in the short term, in institutionalizing a statewide distance learning infrastructure. The roles and activities of project partners have to some degree become codified into Iowa Law and agency decision-making procedures. Consonant with the IDEA Approach, project partners believe that the Iowa Distance Alliance will continue with IPTV facilitating further discussions of partner roles and responsibilities (Sorensen and Sweeney 1994).

All types and levels of educational institutions participate in use of the network, although not without conflict. Private telecommunications companies have so far played a small role, and the process of educational network development has been largely in the hands of educators and state agencies. In other states, the wide variance in existing distance education infrastructures and in the nature and relationships of educational entities, may limit the degree to which Iowa can serve as model; however, the basic approach taken in developing the IDEA could be applied in many different circumstances.

Project Evaluation Measures. Project internal evaluators used a wide variety of techniques to measure progress toward project goals and objectives. They performed formative and summative evaluation activities with stakeholders in all areas of the project, using qualitative and quantitative methods. While the highly decentralized nature of some project activities made data collection and attribution difficult, their overall research plan appears sound and may serve as a model for evaluation of similar comprehensive project efforts in the future.

IDEA-Funded Research Projects. The IDEA funded sixteen studies related to K-12 education and the ICN. Funding research on teaching (or providing release time for research) is one way in which colleges and universities can help faculty in some fields obtain recognition within traditional rewards structures for their teaching at a distance. If some basic parameters are in place, this funded research may add to the overall evaluation efforts of a distance education project.

Reflecting on Project Conclusions and Recommendations

As the internal evaluation study authors concluded, the Star Schools project appears to have been successful in meeting its goals in areas related to the improvement of instructional practices. However, only time will tell whether factors key to the success of the project, such as positive attitudes toward the

ICN, innovative instructional activities, and collaboration among educational organizations, will continue.

Recommendations for future actions in IDEA's Final Evaluation Report included calls for: 1) network expansion; 2) addressing teacher concerns about the need for release time and compensation; 3) development of district, regional, and state policies concerning interactive television teaching in the state; 4) coordination of academic calendars and class schedules, 5) continued teacher training through universities and area education agencies; 6) continued efforts to integrate distance education into preservice teacher education programs; 7) better, perhaps, centralized coordination of information about the system; and 8) continued collaboration and cooperation among educational organizations.

The recommendations for action made by the IDEA in many ways parallel the directions suggested by Moore (1994) in his recent editorial on overcoming the barriers to the establishment of state systems and college and university systems of distance education. They also parallel recommendations of many previous evaluation reports on distance education projects. It is hoped that the research conducted in relation to the Iowa Star Schools project will contribute to efforts to make effective large-scale distance education systems a reality in the United States.

References

Abou-Dagga, S., and M. Herring. 1995. Teacher's training in distance education and their willingness to use the technology after the completion of inservice training. In *Encyclopedia of Distance Education Research*. Ames, IA: IDEA/Research Institute for Studies in Education, Iowa State University.

Baker, M. H. 1995. Distance teaching with interactive television: Strategies that promote interaction with remote-site students. In *Encyclopedia of Distance Education Research*. Ames, IA: IDEA/Research Institute for Studies in Education, Iowa State University.

Brown, F. B., and Y. Brown. 1994. Distance education around the world. In *Distance Education: Strategies and Tools,* ed. B. Willis, 21–39. Cliffs, NJ: Educational Technology Publications.

Fagan, P. J. 1995. Assessment of distance education implementation in Iowa: Concerns and indicators of success. In *Encyclopedia of Distance Education Research*. Ames, IA: IDEA/Research Institute for Studies in Education, Iowa State University.

Hardman, R. 1993. Interactive Television Workshop Guide. Cedar Falls, IA: Center for Education Technology, University of Northern Iowa.

Herring, M. S., S. Smaldino, A. Thompson, and K. Schoenfelder. 1993. Interactive Television Preservice Resource Guidebook. Ames, IA: Teacher Education Alliance/IDEA/Research Institute for Studies in Education, Iowa State University.

IDEA. 1992. IDEA: Partnerships for interactive learning through telecommunications in Iowa's elementary and secondary schools. Grant proposal, USDOE Star Schools Program.

Iowa Public Television. 1994. Fact sheet: ICN. Press release. Johnston, IA: Iowa Public Television.

Kabat, E. J., and J. Friedel. 1990. *The development, pilot-testing, and dissemination of a comprehensive evaluation model for assessing the effectiveness of a two-way interactive distance learning system.* Final Report. Davenport, IA: Eastern Iowa Community College District. ERIC Document Reproduction Service, ED 332 690.

Merkley, D. J., M. Bozik, and K. Oakland. 1995. Investigating teacher change associated with distance learning in education. In *Encyclopedia of Distance Education Research.* Ames, IA: IDEA/Research Institute for Studies in Education, Iowa State University.

Miller, G. 1995. Usefulness of the ICN for delivering instruction in secondary agriculture programs. In *Encyclopedia of Distance Education Research.* Ames, IA: IDEA/Research Institute for Studies in Education, Iowa State University.

Moore, M. G., and M. M. Thompsen. 1990. *The Effects of Distance Learning: A Summary of Literature.* Research Monograph No. 2. University Park, PA: American Center for the Study of Distance Education, The Pennsylvania State University.

Moore, M. G. 1994. Administrative barriers to adoption of distance education. *The American Journal of Distance Education* 8(3):1–4.

Schlosser, C., and M. Anderson. January, 1994. *Distance Education: Review of the Literature.* Washington, DC: Association for Educational Communications and Technology.

Simonson, M., 1993. Interactive study guide: The Iowa philosophy for distance education, November. Unpublished seminar paper.

Simonson, M., J. Sweeney, and M. Kemis, 1993. The IDEA: Star Schools—A special statewide network. *TechTrends* (38)1:25–28, January/February.

Simonson, M., and others. 1992. IDEA: Partnerships for interactive learning through telecommunications in Iowa's elementary and secondary schools. Star Schools grant proposal. Ames, IA: Iowa Distance Education Alliance.

Sorensen, C. K. 1995. Attitudes of community college students toward interactive television instruction. In *Encyclopedia of Distance Education Research*. Ames, IA: IDEA/Research Institute for Studies in Education, Iowa State University.

Sorensen, C. K., C. S. Schlosser, M. Anderson, and M. R. Simonson, eds. 1995. *Encyclopedia of Distance Education Research*. Ames, IA: IDEA/Research Institute for Studies in Education, Iowa State University.

Sorensen, C., and J. Sweeney. December, 1994. IDEA: Final evaluation report. Ames, IA: IDEA/Research Institute for Studies in Education, Iowa State University.

Tushnet, N. C., et al. 1995. Evaluation of the Star Schools Program: Final report. Los Alamitos, CA: Southwest Regional Educational Laboratory for Educational Research and Development.

Tushnet, N. C., et al. 1994. The Star Schools distance-learning program: Results from the mandated study. Paper presented at the Annual Meeting of the American Educational Research Association, New Orleans, LA, April. ERIC Document Reproduction Service, ED 374 149.

4 Analyzing Interaction in Audioconferencing: A Progress Report

Peter S. Cookson

Introduction

Although audioconferencing, i.e., interpersonal voice communication involving people at a minimum of two or more locations via electronic communications technology, has been used as a medium of instruction by North American higher education institutions for decades, systematic empirical research of the process of instruction-learning in audioconferencing situations has not been extensive. The research that has been conducted has been largely descriptive, with a preponderant emphasis on providing a narrative of the overall experience. In relation to studies of audioconferencing, hypothesis-testing has been absent.

One of the key elements to understanding and guiding the nature of instruction by audioconferencing, indeed of multiple forms of distance education, is the concept of *instructional interaction* which typically refers to the interpersonal transactions associated with the processes of education and learning that occur within an instructional setting. Because the few researchers of audioconferencing instruction who have focused on patterns of interaction in audioconferencing have turned to interaction analysis tools more suited to the study of interaction in school class rooms, it could be argued that progress in the in-depth study of instructional interaction in audioconferencing has been retarded. (As we move into an era of expanded use of video teleconferencing, there is lamentably no legacy of developed measures of audioconferencing instruction on which researchers of this newer and more popular mode can build.) It is not surprising that up to now in most of the studies of both audioconferencing and videoconferencing instruction, researchers have been unable to go beyond examination of the structural characteristics (Kirby and Boak 1987) and their own, the instructors' or the participants', overall impressions of the audioconferencing process in which they are engaged.

A fuller treatment of the development of a scale designed to measure interactions in audioconferencing instruction and to thus fill the void was reported by Cookson and Chang (1994). That scale, referred to as the Multidimensional Audioconferencing Classification System (MACS), builds not only on systematic interaction analysis tools developed for systematic observations of instruction in schools, but also on other tools for analysis of small group interaction. Additionally, the MACS builds on features unique to distance education. The result is a scale that sets out to obtain a comprehensive picture of those aspects of teaching and learning reality that are reflected in the verbal interactions transmitted telephonically. The procedures for application of the scale to actual audioconferencing situations are still evolving but the main features of those procedures are now becoming apparent.

The purpose of this paper is to report the ongoing efforts of this researcher to refine the scale so it will be capable of measuring the totality of verbal interactions that occur in audioconferencing instruction. Particular emphasis is given to delineation of the step-by-step procedures interested researchers can follow in applying the model to audioconferencing instruction. Although a number of approaches may be taken to the quantitative analysis of the resulting data, a detailed discussion of the complex statistical analyses such data will require is beyond the scope of this paper. Now that a number of researchers are showing interest in the MACS, it is hoped that detailed procedures for statistical analyses will evolve.

Critical Elements of Interaction in Audioconferencing Instruction

On the basis of their review of the research literature, Cookson and Chang (1994) reported two strands: 1) examination of numerous features of audioconferencing instruction *other than* interaction and 2) examination of interaction in audioconferencing instruction. In their studies of interaction, researchers have been satisfied with using instruments developed to guide observations of interaction in face-to-face education, primarily for school children and youth. Although such instruments capture the salient features of conventional classroom instruction, they also bespeak several limiting assumptions that characterize typical educational settings:

- a dominant teacher
- students who are subordinate to the teacher both chronologically and in terms of unequal power
- a physical classroom
- a reduced range of behavioral categories for both teachers and students.

Anyone using the Flanders' (1970) Systematica Interaction Analysis, for example, cannot escape the baggage accompanying such use. Hence, despite their disarming simplicity of use, in my view, application of the Flanders instrument is inappropriate to the study of audioconferencing interactions in distance education situations that typically involve instructors with participative teaching styles and adult learners whose primary social role is *not* one of *student,* but rather that of *participant.* In short, in addressing those interactional dimensions common to both face-to-face and distance education, an interactional analysis instrument must avoid the limiting assumptions built into the Flanders instrument.

In their quest to go beyond those limiting assumptions, Cookson and Chang (1994) searched for perhaps less known and perhaps more methodologically demanding instruments. We discovered Bales' (1950) pioneering work on small group interaction analysis and Ober, Bentley, and Miller's (1971) Reciprocal Category System. These two instruments suggested interactional categories that are both more diverse and equally applicable to all actors involved in the group—both instructors and students.

But audioconferencing instruction engages conditions other than those shared with face-to-face instruction. Although, over the years many have noted conditions peculiar to audioconferencing instruction, Cookson (1995) has noted four such conditions:

1. Mediation of technology
2. Challenging administrative arrangements for remote sites
3. Geographical dispersal of instructor and learners
4. Absence of visual channel of communication

It is my contention that these conditions, too, must be accounted for by any instrument devised to measure interaction in audioconferencing instruction.

When our focus shifts from the empirical conditions of audioconferencing instruction to the nature of interaction per se in distance education, Moore's (1989) distinctions among three types of interaction comes to mind: learner-content, learner-instructor, and learner-learner. With the property of reciprocity built into the construct of interaction, the order of the interactants named in these three types of interaction may be both unidirectional and bidirectional.

The first type, learner-content interaction, is exemplified by a student's reading and study of a book or printed study guide, listening to an audio-taped lecture, and watching a video-recorded presentation. The content may be structured in such a way as to act upon and/or with the learner. One instructional aim for such interactions is that the learner will engage in what Holmberg (1986, cited in Moore, 1989) refers to as "internal didactic conversation." In audio-conferencing courses, assignments can provide structures for students' interactions with course content prior to and following class sessions. In audioconferencing instruction time may also be set aside for in-class assignments that direct students to relate to course content in specific ways.

The second type, instructor-learner interaction, lies at the core of all distance education programming. It becomes particularly salient in relation to instruction via audioconferencing. Moore describes this form of interaction in terms of the multiple roles of the instructor that involve stimulation, presentation, application, evaluation, and student support (Moore 1989, 4).

The third type, learner-learner interaction, particularly for adult participants, can be a valuable resource for both teaching and learning. Empowered by the instructor, learners may exercise sufficient autonomy to carry out all of the acts normally associated with the instructor—a fact totally ignored by researchers who choose to view audioconferencing instruction through the lenses of the Flanders' (1970) instrument. Learners' interpersonal communications may take such forms as site-group presentations to the entire class, study-teaching teams, mini-course development teams, and site-specific or more general peer group discussions.

Main Features of the MACS

The theoretical model that underlies the Multidimensional Audioconferencing Classification System (MACS) was developed to measure and record instructional interactions in teleconferencing courses. This system represents an effort to go beyond efforts made thus far that have relied on instruments developed primarily for the schooling of children and adolescents. The system is designed to guide the collection of data on both general educational aspects as well as dimensions emerging from distance education aspects of audioconferencing instructional interactions. The *Interactional Dimensions* component of the system expands the Bales Interaction Process Analysis developed by Bales (1950), Ober's reciprocal Category System (Ober 1968; Ober, Bentley, and Miller 1971). The *Distance Education* component of the system expands on an adaptation of Openshaw and Cyphert's Taxonomy of Teacher Behavior (Openshaw and Cyphert 1967), the descriptive and prescriptive literature on audio teleconferencing (Parker and Monson 1980; Burge and Howard 1990; Burge 1991), the sparse research literature on analysis of interaction in teleconferencing instruction (Boak and Kirby 1989), and the authors' experiences since 1987 teaching graduate courses at Penn State via audioconferencing that relate to adult and continuing education as well as distance education.

Figure 1 depicts the theoretical underpinnings of the MACS. The core of the system is the interactional event that, reflected by the *interactional dimensions* as communication, is transmitted from a *source* interactant to a *target* interactant. Additional dimensions that shape interactional dimensions include *focus of the communication, instructional procedures*, and *distance education dimensions*. These elements and dimensions are listed below.

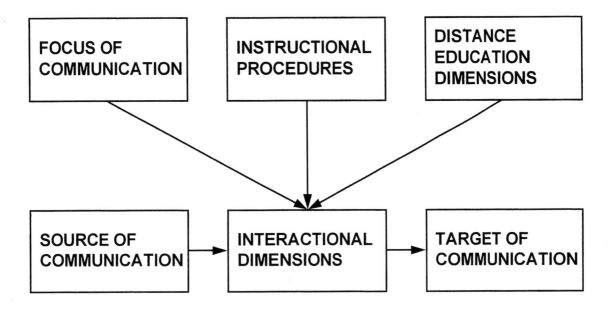

Figure 1. The Multidimensional Audioconferencing Classification System

Table 1 breaks down the specific interactions by general and subordinate sets of dimensions. Instructions for how to apply the MACS are presented in the following section.

Procedure for Applying the MACS

Because the complexity of the classification scheme does not permit analysis of interactions as they occur, the audioconferencing instruction is recorded on audio or videotape and observed three times. Each time different information is noted on the recording sheet. (See Table 2, p. 36) In the first iteration, the observer records the specific interactional dimensions, noting which site talks to which site, leaving for the second iteration the interactants' identity except when the interactant is the instructor. In the second iteration, observers record the identity of specific interactants and, when applicable, specific distance education dimensions. In the third iteration, the time dimension is added by noting the specific counter setting on the playback device for the changes recorded in the two previous iterations.

Table 1. The Multidimensional Audioconferencing Classification System (MACS)

GENERAL ASPECTS	DIMENSION	SPECIFIC INTERACTIONS
I. Interactional Dimensions	a. Social-emotional Dimension: Positive and Mixed	1. SHOWS SOLIDARITY -- raises others' status, gives help and rewards, appears friendly, mentions attributes participants have in common. 2. SHOWS TENSION RELEASE -- informalizes the climate for learning through praises, encourages, expresses satisfaction, laughs, and jokes. 3. AGREES -- shows passive acceptance, understanding of and compliance with contributions of others and provides positive reinforcement. 4. ACKNOWLEDGES -- recognizes another's contribution

	B. Task Area Dimension: Attempted Answers	5. AMPLIFIES THE CONTRIBUTIONS OF ANOTHER -- builds on, and/or develops the action, behavior, comments, ideas and/or contributions of another.
		6. GIVES SUGGESTIONS -- offers alternative ideas/actions and encourages others to explore them, implying autonomy for others.
		7. DIRECTS -- gives directions, instructions, orders, and/or assignments to which another is expected to comply, structures learning activities -- comments that organize learning activities, give assignment.
		8. REACTS TO MAINTAIN LEVEL OF PARTICIPATION -- for example, invites to continue talking to amplify, clarify or summarize ideas at the same or a lower level.
		9. GIVES INFORMATION -- INITIATION -- lectures or presents facts and information about content, subject, or procedures. Ask rhetorical questions that are not intended to be answered.
		10. GIVES INFORMATION -- RESPONDS -- gives direct answers or response to questions or requests for information that are initiated by another; includes answers to one's own questions.
		   a. Responds, restricted (convergent) thinking.
		   b. Responds, broad (divergent) thinking.

	C. Task Area Dimension: Questions	11. ASKS FOR INFORMATION -- elicits information about the content subject, or procedures being considered with the intent that another should respond.
		   a. Asks question eliciting restricted (convergent) thinking.
		   b. Asks question eliciting broad (divergent) thinking.
		12. ASKS FOR OPINION -- asks for another's evaluation, analysis, expression of feeling, or personal opinion or feelings about some topic.
		   a. Asks for a restricted (convergent) thinking response.
		   b. Asks for a broad (divergent) thinking response
		13. ASKS FOR SUGGESTION -- asks for direction, possible ways some task might be performed.
		14. AMPLIFIES OR EXTENDS THE QUESTIONS OF ANOTHER -- asks for clarification of, builds on, and/or develops the statements or questions of another.

	D. Social-emotional Area Dimension: Negative and Mixed	15. DISAGREES -- shows passive rejection, formality, withholds help. 16. CORRECTS -- tells another that his answer or behavior is inappropriate or incorrect. 17. SHOWS TENSION -- asks for help, withdraws out of field. 18. SHOWS ANTAGONISM-- deflates other's status, defends or asserts self, seems unfriendly.
	E. Miscellaneous Dimension	19. SILENCE. 20. CONFUSION.
II. Distance Education Dimensions	a. Administrative Dimension	1. ATTENDANCE -- elicits/records attendance information from all sites. 2. MATERIALS DELIVERY --discusses delivery of instructional materials to participants. 3. TIME/CONTENT MANAGEMENT -- THIS SESSION -- refers to time schedule and/or content outline for this session. 4. TIME/CONTENT MANAGEMENT -- FUTURE -- refers to time schedule and/or content outline for future sessions. 5. LOCAL ARRANGEMENTS -- talks about details of local site access, monitoring, or coordination. 6. OTHER ADMINISTRATIVE MATTERS -- talks or explains about registration/attendance requirements, credit, grades, submission of assignments.

Table 1. Continued

GENERAL ASPECTS	DIMENSION	SPECIFIC INTERACTIONS
	B. Technical Dimension	7. EQUIPMENT -- gives instructions for maintenance, operation, storage, connection, re-connection, back-up systems, and/or trouble shooting of technical equipment. 8. CHECKING OPERATION -- tests, inquires about, or reports status of audio signal for one or more sites. 9. INTERFERENCE WITH AUDIO SIGNAL -- static, distorted sound, uneven signal quality from one or more sites, and/or attempt of participants at two or more sites to speak simultaneously. 10. CONNECTIONS OR RE-CONNECTIONS TO on-line conference -- establishes or re-establishes link to telephone lines and/or audio bridge. 11. LOSS OF AUDIO SIGNAL -- equipment ceases to function and signal ceases from one or more sites.
	C. Visualizing Dimension	12. IMAGERY -- Refers to the content: examples, word pictures, actual situations, personal experience. [In observations column, identify the specific technique used.] 13. REFERENCE TO INSTRUCTIONAL MATERIALS -- talks about materials on hand for most participants. 14. REFERENCE TO VISUAL AIDS -- discusses overhead transparencies, photographs, charts. 15. VISUALIZATION OF VIRTUAL CLASSROOM -- refers to multiple sites; describes current or anticipated presence of participants at multiple sites. 16. VISUALIZATION OF SITE GROUP -- describes a specific site-group setting, responses, actions or attributes of others at the site. 17. PROJECTION OF UPCOMING INVOLVEMENT OF SPECIFIC INDIVIDUALS OR GROUPS -- while engaged in one pattern of interaction, announce a sequence of upcoming involvement in the same session. 18. DISCLOSING OWN IDENTITY. 19. MENTION OF TARGET BY NAME. 20. MONITORING OF GROUP ACTIVITY.
III. Supplemetary Notes	A. Instructional Procedures	1. OVERALL GROUP LEARNING ACTIVITIES 2. SUB-GROUP LEARNING ACTIVITIES 3. INDIVIDUAL LEARNING ACTIVITIES
	B. Miscellaneous	1. TECHNOLOGY -- Employment of specific education technology other than audioconferencing equipment 2. OTHER -- Any unusual occurrence, any activity not addressed by above aspects.

Although ideal circumstances might call for systematic random sampling of equivalent time intervals in an audioconferencing instructional situation, the process of data collection may be made significantly less onerous by observing a time period as small as twenty minutes. Flanders (1970) discovered that a time sample of as little as twenty minutes permitted the determination of an accurate portrayal of a teacher's characteristic teaching behavior. Gorham (1988, 9) describes two other data collection options. One option is point-sampling, whereby "the behavior of each student, in turn, is observed, coded, and recorded—it takes only two to three minutes to point-sample a group of thirty people—with the cycle repeated, in some predetermined order, until sufficient data on each student are obtained. A second option is a "critical event" approach which calls for noting the "behavior for predetermined intervals only following the occurrence of . . . [a particular] critical event."

Table 2. MACS Recording Form

Name, Date, and Time of Program or Event:_____Recorder:_____

A Time	B Who	C To Whom	D Interpersonal Dimensions	E Distance Education Dimensions	F Notes/ Comments

Various approaches may be taken to process and analyze the information recorded on the observation forms, providing answers to many previously difficult-to-answer questions. The columns of codified data must be reduced to numbers that can be subsequently entered into the computer-generated statistical analysis. Interaction patterns may be compared across time periods or with a pattern conceptualized as ideal. Interaction units may be summed into frequencies to permit reporting of how often one kind of interaction was observed over another. When the elapsed time has been recorded, the total time devoted to each behavior can be calculated. Ratios of instructor versus student behaviors may be calculated to permit comparisons of different interaction patterns. A more sophisticated data processing technique, lag analysis (Gorham 1988; Sackett 1978), permits examination of behavioral sequences. This technique permits the examination of cause and effect relationships between and among categories of verbal behaviors. Ratios of instructor versus student behaviors may be calculated to permit comparisons of different interaction patterns. A sample of some of the research questions to be pursued using the MACS is provided below:

- How often did students (fill in the interaction)?
- Did students at the same site as the instructor demonstrate a higher level of verbal activity than students at other sites?
- What proportion of class time was devoted to discussion among students across sites?
- What proportion of class time is devoted to interactions originating with the instructor as opposed to behaviors originating with participants?
- Do participants at the same site as the instructor talk more frequently and for a longer duration than participants at other sites?
- Does instructor-provided action relating to the (name the category here) dimension increase the likelihood of student-initiated responses relating to (name the category here) with participants at other sites?
- What influence on interactional patterns do the following have?
    a. instructor-initiated actions?

    b.   location of origin of certain patterns of interaction?

    c.   social presence of the instructor?

    d.   size of the local site-based group of students?

    e.   cultural and linguistic differences?

    f.   introduction of supplementary technologies (print, audiographics, videoconferencing, computer conferencing)?

    g.   perceptions of local site group environment?

    h.   perceptions of overall group environment?

    i.   distribution of advanced organizers?

    j.   prior involvement of participants in audioconferencing?

    k.   prior involvement of participants in other forms of distance education?

    l.   increasing the number of remote sites?

    m. pre-planning certain kinds of interaction?

    n.   learning style preferences?

    o.   personality type?

    p.   certain forms of interaction?

    q.   individual student characteristics?

- Do instructors and their corresponding groups of students demonstrate a consistent interaction profile?
- How closely do instructor's perceptions of the interaction profile resemble the recorded profile?
- Does informing the instructor of the recorded profile of interactions lead to a change on the instructor's part of the overall class interaction?
- What patterns of interaction are preferred by students? What patterns are perceived to be most instrumental to their learning?
- What patterns of interaction contribute most to:

    a.   a shared sense of group cohesiveness?

    b.   optimal learning?

    c.   sense of satisfaction with audioconferencing?

- Are higher levels of interaction associated with higher levels of learning achievement?
- Can systematic interaction analysis of the teaching-learning process in audioconferencing serve as a needs assessment tool for developing training programs and as an evaluation device?

Next Steps

The next steps in development of this instrument lie in its actual testing for validity and reliability. I know about two ongoing studies involving the use of the MACS: 1) to determine the effects of *transactional distance* (Moore 1980) on different patterns of interaction exhibited by different sites in four countries and 2) to determine the effects of instructors' social presence on participants' patterns of social interaction. My own efforts are devoted to a refinement of what might be regarded as a tedious process of coding observations and application of the system to construct instructors' interactional profiles as a device for staff development and improvement of audioconferencing instruction. Once the instrument has been validated and shown to be reliable, it is anticipated that studies may be mounted to address some of the questions listed in the previous section.

References

Bales, R. F. 1950. A set of categories for the analysis of small group interaction. *American Sociological Review* 15(April):257–263.

Boak, C., and D. Kirby. 1989. Teaching by teleconference: What goes on. In *Proceedings of the Annual Conference of the Canadian Association for the Study of Adult Education,* ed. R. Bedard, 26–32. ERIC Document Reproduction Service, ED 311 202.

Burge, L. 1991. Communicative competence in audio classrooms: A position paper for the CADE 1991 Conference. Paper presented at the Annual Conference of the Canadian Association for Distance Education, Toronto, Ontario, Canada.

Burge, L., and J. Howard. 1990. Audio-conferencing in graduate education: A case study. *The American Journal of Distance Education* 4(2):3–13.

Cookson, P. S. 1995. Instructor and participant responses to critical conditions of audioconferencing. Unpublished manuscript.

Cookson, P. S., and Y. Chang. 1994. The multidimensional audioconferencing classification system (MACS). Paper presented at the International Distance Education Conference, June, University Park, PA.

Flanders, N. A. 1970. *Analyzing Teacher Behavior*. Reading, MA: Addison-Wesley.

Gorham, J. 1988. The relationship between verbal teacher immediacy behaviors and student learning. *Communication Education* 37:40–53.

Holmberg, B. 1986. *Growth and Structure of Distance Education*. London: Croom Helm.

Kirby, D., and C. Boak. 1987. Developing a system for audio-teleconferencing analysis (SATA), *Journal of Distance Education* 2:31–42.

Moore, M. G. 1980. Independent study. In *Redefining the Discipline of Adult Education,* eds. R. Boyd, J. Apps, and Associates, 16–31. San Francisco: Jossey-Bass.

Moore, M. G. 1989. Three types of interaction. The American Journal of Distance Education 3(2)1–7.

Ober, R. L. 1968. *The Reciprocal Category System.* Morgantown, WV: West Virginia University.

Ober, R., E. Bentley, and E. Miller. 1971. *Systematic Observation of Teaching.* Englewood Cliffs, NJ: Prentice-Hall.

Openshaw, M. K., and F. R. Cyphert. 1967. Taxonomy of teacher behavior. In *Mirrors for Behavior III: An Anthology of Observation Instruments,* eds. A. Simon and E. G. Boyer, 461–66. Devon, PA: Anro Press.

Parker, L. A., and M. K. Monson. 1980. *Teletechniques: An Instructional Model for Interactive Teleconferencing.* Englewood Cliffs, NJ: Educational Publications.

Sackett, G. P. 1978. Measurement in observational research. In *Observing Behavior, Volume II: Data Collection and Analysis Methods,* ed. P. Sackett. Baltimore: University Park Press.

<table>
| 5 | **Teaching in Two Environments: A Case Study Comparing Face-To-Face and On-Line Instruction** |
</table>

Patricia González

Introduction

Computer-mediated communication (CMC) combines the benefits of group dynamics with the freedom associated with time and place independence. In this way, CMC opens new possibilities for teaching and learning that draw on strengths of both face-to-face and distance education (Harasim 1989). Group processes can be a part of distance education (Nipper 1989), and traditional institutions can reach a broader student population. The boundaries between traditional and distance education become blurred (Kaye 1989), and concepts that were central to face-to-face instruction—like classroom interaction—become relevant in a new way. A new set of relations among learners, instructors and content seems to emerge on-line. Theorists refer to a new domain (Harasim 1989), a paradigm (Kaye 1989; Mason and Kaye 1990), or a distinct environment (Roberts 1988) depending on their assessment of the nature and impact of the qualitative differences of these emerging relations. While collaboration, constructivism, and democracy are highlighted throughout the literature on CMC, there is little evidence that other teaching models are not viable in this environment. This paper discusses a course developed using a noncollaborative model, taught in the face-to-face environment and on-line. Factors that affect classroom interaction, both medium and non-medium related, are explored.

Computer-Mediated Communication and Teaching

A widely accepted basis for the analysis of CMC is Harasim's list of attributes of the medium: 1) many-to-many communication; 2) place independence; 3) time independence; 4) text-based; 5) computer-mediated interaction (Harasim 1990). Related to these attributes, a series of qualities of the medium have been presented: a more democratic environment (Roberts 1988; Harasim 1989; Kaye 1989: Florini 1991; Lewis and Hedegaard 1993; Jonassen 1994), enhanced collaboration and constructivism (Roberts 1988; Harasim 1989; Kaye 1989; Florini 1991; Wells 1993; Tagg 1994), reflective thinking (Roberts 1988; Harasim 1989; Kaye 1989; Lewis and Hedegaard 1993), and an enriched environment (Roberts 1988; Kaye 1989; Florini 1991; Tuckey 1993), as well as some limitations: difficult decision-making (Harasim 1989; Tuckey 1993), limited sharing of knowledge (Roberts 1988), problems of coherence, and need for moderation (Davie 1989; Roberts 1988; Feenberg 1989; Florini 1991).

In relation to teaching, a common claim in the literature has been that the teaching models which place the teacher/tutor as the source of knowledge should give way to: 1) models where peer support and collaboration is emphasized (Harasim 1990), or 2) models where the process is centered in linking learners to information sources (Lanfranco and Utsumi 1993). Factors for predicting the success of on-line teachers and facilitators have included "a commitment to the values of group work and cooperative learning" (Kaye 1989, 15). Instructors are encouraged to adopt facilitative or moderating roles (Wells 1993), and to pass on moderating responsibilities to students (Tagg 1994). Although experience has shown these collaborative and constructivist approaches to learning have worked in the on-line environment (Harasim 1989; Davie 1989), there is little evidence that other models cannot be used successfully (Florini 1991). Four years ago, in this same forum (The Second American Symposium on Research in Distance Education) Barbara Florini stressed the need for qualitative case studies that described and reported the use of different models.

So, while the list of attributes and recommendations has informed research and practice in the field, it has often failed to distinguish what CMC does (the theoretical nature of the medium) from what CMC can do (its potential applications) and how CMC should be used (the implications for practice). Although the literature highlights democracy, collaboration, and reflective thinking as qualities of CMC, recent studies show that they are not intrinsic to the medium (Burge 1993; Eastmond 1994), but that they are determined by other factors such as course design, teaching philosophy, and participation patterns (Burge 1993; Eastmond 1994). There is a need to differentiate the effects of the medium from curriculum design and teaching/learning philosophy. Suggestions for practice relative to particular teaching models can then be raised.

Research Problem and Methodology

The case study in this paper depicts the delivery of a sociology course taught by the same instructor in two environments: face-to-face and on-line. Classroom interaction in both environments is discussed in order to explore the factors that affected the relationship between teacher and learners. The following questions guided the analysis: How does classroom interaction change on-line as compared to the face-to-face environment? What factors determine these differences? Are these factors related to the attributes of the medium? Classroom interaction was defined as reciprocal events that take place between the learning and the learning environment (Wagner 1994), and it was limited to teacher-student and student-student interaction according to Moore's typology (1989).

An ethnographic methodology was selected. Data was gathered through participant observation of each course (six sessions of the face-to-face class; four weeks of interaction in the on-line version), journal notes, interviews with the teacher and open-ended student questionnaires (a small return was obtained: 55% from face-to-face students; 62%, on-line). Patterns of talk were identified in the data and categories were construed and contrasted with issues that appear in the literature. Finally, both data and its interpretation were presented to the teacher for validation purposes.

A coding system was not used in order to avoid imposing specific assumptions on the data (Walker and Adelman 1993). Although generalization of findings might be limited, flexible observations were selected for their value in generating useful perspectives about the impact of different teaching models in CMC.

Institutional Context. The Sociology of Identity course was developed as part of The New School for Social Research's initiative1 to explore the use of technology for the delivery of an interdisciplinary humanities curriculum. In the fall of 1993, it was offered in the face-to-face format; during the spring of 1994, it was implemented on-line. Two other courses were taught in the same time frame in both environments. Registration was limited to undergraduate credit students from The New School's bachelor's degree program. As a completion program, it serves a student population of adult learners, with an average age of thirty-five to forty years and typically two-thirds of which are females. In this course, nine students (two of them male) were enrolled in the classroom version, and eight (one of them male) were in the on-line version. Special discounted fees were established for the course. The teacher and students in both formats consented to the observation of classroom interaction.

Technology. The on-line course was taught using PARTICIPATE as a computer-conferencing system. In the course conference, messages were posted linearly and chronologically, and no branches were used. Searching tools and private e-mail were available. Connection costs were covered by The New School (except for local calls to access numbers). Students had to provide the computer, modem, and communications software.

Teacher and students were trained in the use of the technology. The teacher observed an on-line course and participated in an on-line teaching workshop and an on-line discussion forum with two other prospective instructors. A technical handbook was prepared for students, and they participated in a one week training workshop that covered basic technical tasks: reading and writing messages, uploading and downloading.

Course Structure. The teacher designed the course for both environments, trying to keep curricular differences to a minimum. A loosely structured syllabus was used in both environments: general goals for the course were established, the three canonical texts were listed, and explicit deadlines for the three papers were stipulated. For the face-to-face course, supplementary readings were placed on reserve in the school's library; for the on-line version, they were mailed to the students. The face-to-face course consisted of thirteen 105 minute sessions; the on-line version comprised eight weeks of asynchronous interaction.

Teaching Philosophy, Teaching Strategies, and Classroom Interaction

The overall goal as described by the teacher was to teach the students to think analytically. Two specific objectives were pursued: 1) "to expose the students to important works on identity and to lay out the argument on what we mean by identity," and 2) "to show them the way in which our idea of identity has dramatically changed in a postmodern age." The teacher identified her role as a mediator between the texts studied and the students. Her knowledge of the texts made it possible for her "to clarify the material, to make very abstract and turgid material come to life." Her understanding of the students' experience enabled her to present relevant examples; her passion for the subject helped her convey the importance of the texts to the students. Teaching and learning were associated with exposure to information. This philosophy of adult education can be related to the liberal perspective as defined by White and Brockett's typology (Zinn 1990).

In both formats of the course, the teacher relied on lectures and recitation as teaching strategies. Recitation is used here in Dillon's terms (1988) to identify the classroom interaction characterized by the teacher presenting questions with predetermined answers in mind. A cognitive plan has been chartered and thus, this kind of exchange is not directed to a collective search for answers. It cannot be defined as true discussion because it has lost its democratic nature (Brookfield 1990).

Face-to-face. The face-to-face sessions started with a lecture in which the teacher presented the main ideas of the texts, related them to other authors, pointed out areas to be thought out by students, and illustrated how the concepts could be applied. The presentation of examples opened a space for students' comments and a series of exchanges ensued between the teacher and students. The teacher mediated student participation: she responded to a comment and acknowledged or selected the next speaker. The pattern of talk was T-S-T-S-T-S (where each letter is an utterance and S can represent any student). In her interventions, the teacher encouraged controversy by posing radical questions, taking extreme positions, and giving polemic answers. She also examined the student's comment, invited analysis of the position stated, or rephrased the idea. Students' comments were short (one or two sentences), informal (unfinished phrases, slang, colloquial expressions), and they were addressed to the teacher. Student-student interaction was scarce, and even when it took place, the students looked for the teacher's reaction. Two tones can be differentiated in the teacher's participation. While she lectured, sometimes reading from her notes, her discourse was theoretical and formal. When she illustrated concepts and participated in exchanges with students, she used irony, humor, swear words, slang, and colloquialisms. There was a change in the proportion of lecture and recitation in the sessions. The prolonged recitation periods and short lectures gave way to longer lectures and less exchange in the final classes.

On-line. In the on-line course, the teacher used long lecture-messages with similar objectives as her live lectures. She inserted questions throughout the message to promote students' reflection, and at the end of the message she presented specific issues for students to comment upon.

Although there was not a formal turn-taking process (since the floor is opened to all on-line), a pattern of interaction can be identified. The teacher's lecture set a topic to be analyzed. As students' responses came in, the teacher gave feedback to each of them. In some cases, she related the student's ideas with the arguments of the authors, thus, the responses were used to make a point and woven into the main conversation. At other times, the teacher's feedback gave rise to a parallel line of conversation that was continued by the teacher and the respective student. The teacher presented new material without waiting for student responses. A pattern of dialogue emerged in which the teacher led and participated in multiple threads of conversation. In the latter part of the course, students referred to each other's comments and joined in the simultaneous discussion threads.

The teacher generally dedicated each message to a single objective, sometimes posting several messages one after the other. Lecture messages were long (over 1000 words); assignments or additional reflections on a topic were shorter (300-800) words. Feedback to students was identified with the initials of the addressee; different kinds of feedback varied in length (100-500 words). Answers to practical issues were short and to the point (1-150 words). One predominant tone was used in the teacher's messages: a conversational but very formal, academic discourse. Humor, irony, provocation, and personal stories were absent.

Students' comments also varied according to their purpose. Messages for technical issues and class management were short and to the point. Answers to assignments/questions or comments on readings were longer (100-800 words). They were formally written—like short essays—and presented the student's opinion, applied concepts to personal experience, provided additional examples, or posed related questions. During the first month, students only responded to the teacher's comments; in the second half of the course, they made occasional references to each others' responses.

The Written Persona

An analysis of the differences and similarities in the classroom interaction in each environment makes it possible to explore factors that affected the delivery of the course in both environments. First, there is a drastic difference in the tone of the teacher's discourse. The provocative and challenging comments used in the face-to-face format disappeared. So did the irony and the humor. Whereas in the classroom she posed informal questions, in her on-line lectures she distanced herself. Comments that were considered suitable to be said in the classroom were deemed inappropriate to be written.

The teacher relates her change in tone to two factors: anxiety towards the technology and her expectations that her writing be formal. Yet, although her fears were reduced as she interacted with students, her consistent tendency toward the formal tone is apparent.

A Public, No Nonsense Environment

A difference in the nature of the examples selected for each environment also stands out. Polemic issues—and radical positions, "the devil's advocate"—were frequently taken up by the teacher in the face-to-face environment. On-line, the teacher illustrated concepts with "safer" issues. Some of the attributes of the medium influenced the teacher's selection of topics. The lack of visual cues and the time delay in students' responses made the teacher afraid of being offensive. The teacher was also aware that in the on-line environment the existence of a transcript affects the private nature of classroom interaction: "There's a kind of censorship... I was much more restrained than I was in the earlier class and I think it's because on-line is for public consumption."

Personal stories were frequently used in the face-to-face environment for a specific pedagogical purpose: to loosen up the students. On-line they were deemed inappropriate and leading to chatter. The on-line interaction she observed in another course had struck her as chat and as a result, she was concerned about the level of discussion in her own course.

Pacing

In each environment, changes in the interaction over time highlight other effects of the medium in the delivery of the course. In the initial face-to-face sessions, short lectures were followed by long periods of recitation. There were frequent digressions from the initial topic as additional examples were brought in by the teacher and students. Content was covered slowly. After the fourth session, the teacher lectured longer. Students' comments and questions were reduced. One of the books was not analyzed completely. Pacing was identified by the teacher as one of her challenges in the classroom: "I've always said I could perfect my own teaching. I just get sidetracked very early on in my class by their questions and in part it's because I know they love to be involved."

The on-line class developed differently. The teacher's lectures were evenly distributed throughout the course. The teacher was not interrupted by visual digressions and thus, her tendency to diverge decreased. The syllabus was covered completely. Students participation increased with time. An additional benefit of the separation in time and place from her students was that the teacher could bring external resources into her lectures: "I was able to write very effective conversational lectures because I can pause and pull a book from the shelf. So there is a polish to those lectures that I just don't do when I teach live."

Student Participation

Students' responses in the two environments show differences and similarities. In the face-to-face, some students participated intensively in lively discussions directed by the instructor. Although students' contributions were not timed, the pattern of interaction identified by the observer was confirmed by the instructor: classroom interaction tended to be dominated by one student, four students participated regularly and three tended to remain silent. As it was mentioned before, students' comments were short and informally structured.

A similar distribution in students' participation was identified on-line. There were 158 messages in the course; 61% were attributed to the teacher; four students contributed with 36%; two students with 3% ; and one student did not participate (but successfully completed the course). As the course progressed the proportion changed. In the first quarter of the course, the teacher posted 77% of the messages; in the second, 69%; in the third, 51%; and 56% in the fourth. These figures illustrate partially the predominant nature of teacher. On-line, topic-related participation from students was not limited to short, spontaneous comments as in face-to-face interaction, and it was characterized by reflective thinking: "It made me think more when I made a comment." Messages were carefully written and structured as short essays. Consequently, on two occasions the teacher was confused about whether a student's messages was a response or an actual paper.

Distribution of classroom participation followed similar patterns in both environments: the teacher filled up talk-time, and classroom interaction was dominated by a core group of students. Student-student interaction was very limited in both environments. In the face-to-face format, students confronted each other's positions in the recitation periods yet conversation was mediated by the teacher. On-line student messages tended to respond to teacher assignments or questions. An interesting issue, though, is how students' perception of other students' participation changed in each format. In the face-to-face class, none of the students were disturbed by the unequal participation of students. They valued other students' comments as diverse perspectives and sources of knowledge. Nevertheless, four on-line students mentioned the fact that some students participate more than others. While for three of them, their classmates participation was valuable, one found it "out of context at times," and another student complained that "some students like to hear themselves talk."

Students' comments make it possible to explore factors that influenced their participation on-line: technical problems and comfort with their own writing. Four students mentioned that technical difficulties made them feel uncomfortable on-line. For three of them, the discomfort disappeared as they became familiar with the system. Nevertheless, for one student, "poor typing skills, technical problems and the labor involved did away with any possibility for spontaneous discussion." Students' insecurity about their writing skills was an inhibiting factor. However, two students also mentioned that as a result of the course, their writing improved.

Implications for Theory

The analysis of classroom interaction shows how the teacher had to adapt to the on-line environment in order to put into practice her teaching philosophy. Since her goal was related to exposure of information and student participation was only secondary, she used lecture and recitation as teaching strategies in both cases. On-line her tone became more formal and her topics less controversial and less personal. Students' participation changed from intense contributions with many short unstructured comments during the face-to-face recitation periods, to a few long, structured messages on-line. In both environments, only a small group of students participated and student-student interaction was scarce.

It is interesting to note that although similar relations were established in both environments (centered on the teacher as the source of knowledge and students as receivers), the teacher's and the students' positions were affected by the medium. In her studies of face-to-face interaction, Delamont (1986) described how the teacher's position in front of a group was characterized by three traits: privacy (since s/he is in a closed space: the classroom), immediacy (because s/he has to respond immediately), and autonomy (s/he has to decide on her/his own how to react). While teaching on-line, asynchronicity gave the teacher the opportunity to rely on additional resources that strengthened her control over knowledge. Transcripts, though, challenged the privacy of the interaction and made her feel more vulnerable.

The change in the position of the students is not so clear. An important fact is that although student participation had similar patterns of distribution in both environments, students' perception of participation varied. Only on-line students were disturbed by the unequal rates of participation in the class. Thus, while equality might not be inherent in the on-line environment, students tend to be more aware of the differences in participation. This issue requires further study. An interesting approach would be to explore how spaces for resistance (in Giroux's terms) or negotiation (Apple) conform in the on-line classroom.

This case study demonstrates that the attributes of computer conferencing do not necessarily lead to a more egalitarian environment as often assumed in the literature. The medium, while clearly influential, is in service to the teacher's and students' use. Attitude and belief about the condition of the environment and teaching and learning philosophy play important roles in the equation. Clearly, there is a need for further research to contrast experiences where different teaching philosophies and technical platforms are used to teach a variety of subjects. A composite of studies will be helpful to understand the dynamics in multiple contexts and to distinguish the effects of the medium from the specificities of the educational setting.

References

Burge, E. 1993. Author's comment reporting findings of her dissertation project: Students Perceptions of Learning in Computer Conferencing: A Qualitative Analysis. (UnM AAINN82689)

Brookfield, S. 1990. Discussion. In *Adult Learning Methods,* ed. M. Galbraith, 187–204. Malabar: Krieger.

Davie, L. 1989. Facilitation techniques for the on-line tutor. In *Mindweave, Communications, Computers and Distance Education,* eds. R. Mason and A. Kaye, 74–85. Oxford: Pergamon Press.

Delamont, S. 1986. *Interaction in the Classroom.* London: Routledge.

Dillon, J. T. 1988. *Questioning and Teaching: A Manual of Practice.* New York: Teachers College.

Eastmond, D. 1994. Adult distance study through computer conferencing. *Distance Education* 15(1):128–52.

Feenberg, A. 1989. The written world. In *Mindweave, Communications, Computers and Distance Education,* eds. R. Mason and A. Kaye, 22–39. Oxford: Pergamon Press.

Florini, B. 1991. Course design in on-line distance education: A paper for discussion. In Discussion Papers for the Second American Symposium on Research in Distance Education. University Park, PA: The Pennsylvania State University.

Harasim, L. 1989. Online education: A new domain. In *Mindweave, Communications, Computers and Distance Education,* eds. R. Mason and A. Kaye, 50–62. Oxford: Pergamon Press.

Harasim, L. 1990. Online education: An environmnet for collaboration and intellectual amplification. In *Online Education: Perspectives on a New Environment,* ed. L. Harasim, 39–64. New York: Praeger.

Jonassen, D. H. 1994. Conceptual models for structuring computer-mediated collaborative knowledge of construction. Discussion Paper for the International Distance Education Conference. University Park, PA: The Pennsylvania State University.

Kaye, A. 1989. CMC and Distance Education. In *Mindweave, Communications, Computers and Distance Education,* eds. R. Mason and A. Kaye, 3–21. Oxford: Pergamon Press.

Lanfranco, S., and T. Utsumi. 1993. Objects, agents and events in a global learning environment. Discussion Paper for Teleteaching '93. Trondheim, Norway.

Lewis, C. T., and T. Hedegaard. 1993. Online education: Issues and some answers. *THE Journal,* April 1993:68–71.

Mason, R., and T. Kaye. 1990. Toward a new paradigm for distance edcuation. In *Online Education: Perspectives on a New Environment,* ed. L. Harasim, 15–38. New York: Praeger.

Moore, M. G. 1989. Three types of interaction. *The American Journal of Distance Education* 3(2):1–6.

Nipper, S. 1989. Third generation distance learning and computer conferencing. In *Mindweave, Communications, Computers and Distance Education,* eds. R. Mason and A. Kaye, 63–73. Oxford: Pergamon Press.

Roberts, L. 1988. Computer conferencing: A classroom for distance learning. *ICDE Bulletin* 18:35–40.

Tagg, A. 1994. Leadership from within: Student moderation of computer conferences. *The American Journal of Distance Education* (8)3:40–50.

Tuckey, C. J. 1993. Computer conferencing and the electronic white board. *The American Journal of Distance Education* 7(2):58–72.

Walker, R., and C. Adelman. 1993. Interaction analysis in informal classrooms: A critical comment on the Flanders system. In *Controversies in Classroom Research,* ed. M. Hammersley, 3–9. Buckingham: Open University Press.

Wagner, E. 1994. In support of a functional definition of interaction. *The American Journal of Distance Education* 8(2):6–29.

Wells, R. 1993. *Computer-Mediated Communication for Distance Education: An International Review of Design, Teaching, and Institutional Issues.* Research Monograph No. 6. University Park, PA: American Center for the Study of Distance Education.

Zinn, L. M. 1990. Identifying your philosophical orientation. In *Adult Learning Methods,* ed. M. Galbraith, 44–79. Malabar: Krieger.

Note: This experience was partially funded by the U.S. Department of Education, Fund for the Improvement of Post-Secondary Education.

6 An Examination of Teaching and Learning Processes in Distance Education and Implications for Designing Instruction

Charlotte N. Gunawardena and Rebecca Zittle

Introduction

In any educational transaction, teaching and learning are inextricably linked. Garrison (1993) observes that assumptions regarding learning are implicit in designs of instruction and education, and points out that "If the goal of distance education is to facilitate learners in their construction of meaning then methods, materials, and evaluation must be congruent with that goal" (p. 208). A comprehensive review of the literature on distance teaching (Dillon and Walsh 1992) identifies teaching techniques that have been shown to increase student satisfaction and perceptions of learning. These are "immediacy behaviors" such as addressing students by name, encouraging discussion and verbal or written contact, vocal variety, praise, smiling, and a relaxed body posture. Successful strategies identified are almost invariably those that provide for maximum interaction among students and between students and the instructor. Examples of these are the use of structured question and answer sessions, group activities, effective verbal and nonverbal presentation methods, using silence to encourage reflection, and careful organization and management of materials and the learning environment. Two themes related to effective distance instruction emerged naturally from the literature. These are: 1) teaching and learning processes and related distance teaching strategies and techniques, and 2) changes in faculty roles in the distance teaching environment.

Purpose of This Study

The purpose of this paper is to review recent literature on teaching and learning processes in distance education and to discuss implications for the design of effective distance instruction. The paper will analyze teaching and learning principles that emerged from the literature: 1) learner-centered instruction, 2) interaction, 3) social presence, 4) cognitive strategies, and 5) collaborative learning, and examine role changes that distance instructors adopt or have to adopt in order to facilitate learning at a distance. The discussion of literature in each of the five categories will include implications for improving practice. This paper will conclude with a framework for planning distance instruction and suggestions for future research.

Method

This review of literature focuses predominantly on papers published since 1992, as Dillon and Walsh (1992) conducted a comprehensive survey of issues related to distance instruction that was published in *The American Journal of Distance Education*. Sources for the present study were selected from refereed journals, non-refereed journals, ERIC reports, technical reports on Star Schools evaluations submitted to the U.S. Department of Education, and papers available through the World Wide Web. Articles from the following journals were selected for this study: *The American Journal of Distance Education, British Journal of Educational Technology, Distance Education, Educational Technology Research and Development, Journal of Distance Education, Open Learning,* and *Technical Horizons in Education.* The majority of articles and research papers examined are either descriptions of single programs or anecdotal evidence of teaching experience. Very few articles provided empirical evidence on the effectiveness of specific teaching strategies.

Review of Literature on Teaching and Learning Processes

The review of literature on teaching and learning processes and implications for practice are discussed under the following themes that emerged from the review of literature: 1) learner-centered instruction, 2) interaction, 3) social presence, 4) cognitive strategies, and 5) collaborative learning. While role changes for distance instructors related to each of these themes are discussed in each section, a separate section on changes in faculty roles takes a more in-depth look at changes that distance instructors adopt in order to facilitate learning at a distance.

Learner-Centered Instruction. It is difficult to determine whether the shift to more learner-centered instruction is driven by the technology or by instructors bringing such an orientation with them to the distance education context. The literature appears to support both viewpoints. To cite support for the first hypothesis, Moore (1993) draws analogies between distance education and other fields in the early stages of their evolution, such as film-making. To realize the potential of the new technology it was necessary for practitioners to do more than point the camera at the stage; a reorganization of the design and implementation of film-making was necessary to advance it to its current state. Support from the field comes from faculty who observe that the learner-centered techniques and strategies they adopt when teaching at a distance transfer positively to their traditional classroom situations and make them more effective teachers (Catchpole 1992; Dillon and Walsh 1992; Boston 1992).

In support of the second hypothesis is the literature concerning those instructors who, with or without the aid of program developers, approach the initial design of their courses from a learner-centered orientation (Worley 1993; Schmidt, Sullivan, and Hardy 1994). A pilot program to teach algebra to migrant students that was designed using a constructivist approach indicates that a learner-centered course can very effectively deliver difficult concepts such as algebra even via low-end technology such as audioconferencing (Schmidt, Sullivan, and Hardy 1994).

Gunawardena (1992) observes that instructional designs must address the complex interrelationships between learning task, media attributes and the learner's cognitive processes. Two-way interactive telecommunication systems provide opportunities to develop learner-controlled instructional systems that make frequent interaction mandatory for effective learning experiences. Describing her teaching experience using an audiographics system, Gunawardena (1992) discusses the design of a learner-centered graduate course where the focus was on learner initiated inquiry and exploration. She observes that she had to change her role from that of a teacher in front of the classroom to a facilitator who is one with the participants and whose primary role is to guide and support the learning process.

Future research should focus on the interaction between learner-centered learning environments and learner achievement and transfer of learning. Questions that need to be addressed are: Do learner-centered learning environments promote transfer of learning? Which aspects of such learning environments or which design elements promote transfer of learning?

Interaction. The issue of 'interaction' has been an area of much debate in the practice of distance education. Wagner (1994) points out that the terms 'interaction' and 'interactivity' are often used without paying much attention to what they actually mean and makes a distinction between two categories of interaction. These are: interactions which are the property of learning events, and delivery system interactions which are properties of media. She argues that interaction functions as an attribute of effective instruction, while interactivity functions as an attribute of contemporary instructional delivery systems and points out that when distance educators discuss interaction, often their focus is on the attributes and outcomes of real-time, two-way exchange of information.

Examining instructional interaction, Moore (1989) makes a distinction between three types of interaction: learner-content interaction, learner-instructor interaction, and learner-learner interaction. The interaction between the learner and content is the process of intellectually interacting with content that results in changes in the learner's understanding, perspective, or the cognitive structures of the learner's mind. The second type is the interaction between the learner and the instructor, a type of interaction that is regarded as essential by many educators and highly desired by many learners. The third type of interaction, is the interaction that takes place between one learner and other learners, alone or in group settings, either in the presence or absence of an instructor, and it is this type of interaction that would contribute immensely to a learner-centered view of learning.

Hillman, Willis, and Gunawardena (1994) argue that Moore's (1989) three types of interaction do not account for all aspects of interaction in technology-mediated distance education. They point out that the addition of high technology communications systems necessitates the conceptualization of an additional type of interaction: learner-interface interaction. They note that a facet of distance education that is increasingly overlooked is the effect of high-technology devices on interaction. Instructors and learners have to interact with the technology and manipulate interfaces in order to be able to communicate with each other. In order to address the learner-interface problem, they suggest three types of activities to make the learner and instructor at ease with the technology. These include in-class exercises, orientation sessions, or technology credit courses.

Future research should shed light on the following questions: What type and level of interaction is essential for effective learning? How can we achieve interaction? What does real-time and time-delayed interaction contribute? What type of interaction can the new interactive technologies provide? Is it worth the cost?

Social Presence. Dede (1989) observes that successful distance instruction depends on more than classroom management strategies, knowledge of subject matter, pedagogical expertise, and the ability to use the technology. The ability to create an intellectually and emotionally attractive "telepresence" and the ability to build "virtual communities" of learners are also vital skills for a distance instructor. Telepresence or "social presence" is defined by Short, Williams, and Christie (1976) as the "degree of salience of the other person in the interaction and the consequent salience of the interpersonal relationships..." (p. 65). This means the degree to which a person is perceived as a "real person" in mediated communication.

Hackman and Walker's (1990) study provides evidence that "teacher immediacy" contributes to student satisfaction and learning in an interactive television class. They argue that there are differences between telecommunications delivered instruction and traditional face-to-face instruction, specifically in terms of the climate of "social presence" created. Walther (1992) cites research which suggests that social presence can "be cultured" among teleconference participants, a position different from the view that social presence is largely an attribute of the communication medium. Research has indicated that computer-mediated communication (CMC) users in particular develop an ability to express missing nonverbal cues in written form. Therefore, studying a medium from a relational communication perspective offers an approach to the process that differs from a channel-effects view alone. A relational perspective suggests that functional and social factors should be examined.

Gunawardena (1995) discusses a study which examined students' subjective perceptions of CMC after participation in the Globaled computer conference that linked graduate students in several universities to engage in collaborative learning activities. The results indicate that despite CMC's low social context cues, students perceived it as an interactive, active, interesting, and stimulating medium. However, it is the kind of interactions that take place between the participants, and the sense of community that is created during the conference, that will impact participants' perceptions of CMC as a "social" medium.

Future research should examine telecommunications-based learning environments from a relational perspective and determine the degree of social presence necessary for affective and cognitive learning. As Walther (1992) has pointed out it is also important to determine whether the actual characteristics of the media are the causal determinants of communication differences or whether users' perceptions of media alter their behavior. Future research should attempt to determine to what extent the degree of social presence, social context, or the relational qualities associated with a medium such as CMC may be affected by the different social processes, settings, and purposes within CMC use.

Cognitive Strategies. Gagne, Briggs, and Wager (1988) state that a cognitive strategy is a "control process," an internal process by which learners select and modify their ways of attending, learning, remembering, and thinking. West, Farmer, and Wolff (1991, 22) define cognitive strategies as "mental activities performed by persons," and that learning these strategies is aided by their incorporation into instruction. They observe that cognitive strategies may be grouped into four families: chunking or organizing strategies such as complex arrays or frames, spatial learning strategies such as concept maps, bridging strategies such as advance organizers and metaphors, and general purpose strategies which include rehearsal, imagery, and mnemonics. West, Farmer, and Wolff (1991) cite research which provides evidence that concept mapping is especially useful when students construct concept maps after or during the study of content, and when knowledge of concepts and relationships is the primary goal of instruction. The medium of television lends itself well to imagery. It can provide mental pictures to those who are unable to create images on their own. Salomon (1983) considers this visual "supplantation" the most important function of television's pictorial characteristics, and observes that it facilitates learning when images so supplanted are of ongoing multivariate novel processes.

In her study of twenty adults enrolled in an independent study course, Olgren (1992) found that learners used cognitive strategies to construct meaning and knowledge from text. The study identified four types of cognitive strategies: 1) selection strategies, of which there are two types: (i) external, which focus on identifying information in the textbook considered to be important by the author or instructor, and (ii) internal, which focus on the learner's needs and identifying information of importance and interest to the learner; 2) rehearsal strategies to aid retention; 3) organization strategies to build connections within the text, and 4) elaboration strategies to expand meaning and build connections to prior knowledge and experience. The achievement of deeper levels of learning involved active mental engagement through higher-level cognitive strategies as well as emotional engagement stimulated by the learner's personal goals and perceptions of the value of the task. The employment of various strategies was found to be influenced by a combination of strategy knowledge, learner's perceptions and interpretations of the task, motivations, and past experience of academic study.

Future research should further examine the variables studied by Olgren (1992), and determine which cognitive strategies enhance learning from different forms of mediated communication.

Collaborative Learning. Until the advent of communications technologies that are capable of facilitating two-way interaction, arranging collaborative learning and group work among distance learners has been a difficult task. Research has indicated that collaborative group work can increase motivation, completion rates, student satisfaction, and depending on the number of students in the group, even performance (Wells 1990). Dillenbourg et al. (n.d.) observe that attaining shared understanding of meanings of utterances is a necessary condition for collaborative work. Without a communication medium other than the telephone with implied long distance costs that students are capable of using, facilitating groups at a distance can be frustrating. While CMC is an excellent communication medium, if students do not have easy access to it or do not have the training to use it, it would be of no use as a communication link. Discussing Computer Supported Cooperative Work

(CSCW), Dede (1989) observes that one useful feature for bridging geographic and temporal barriers to teamwork at a distance is an intelligent agent that the user can program to filter and organize information. He notes that the Lens Project in the Sloan School of Management at MIT illustrates the use of these intelligent agents in a research setting.

In the Technical Education Research Center (TERC) Star Schools evaluation report, Weir, Krensky, and Gal (1990) observe that students reported qualitative differences in the way collaborative arrangements were implemented in the traditional and distance settings. The collaboration in the traditional class was described as usually organized around the teacher, who often controlled the communication process. In contrast, they preferred the setup in the Star Schools Units, where teams were felt to be more self-managed, with greater and more open interaction among the students and with more group generated input rather than reliance on external information sources.

Future research should examine the following questions: What opportunities are presented by various media for collective learning and peer exchange? How does the on-line environment affect group interaction? How do group dynamics impact peer exchange and collaborative learning? How do conferencing systems support three educational processes: idea generating (and gathering), idea linking, and idea structuring? In studying collaborative learning and group dynamics in various distance education environments, it is important to consider variables such as the communications medium, degree of cooperation, how the group organizes itself, and how the dynamics of group cooperation are achieved.

Changes in Faculty Roles

Distance education's evolution to a learner-centered view of learning and the need to utilize a variety of new telecommunications technologies to promote such learning, requires dramatic changes in the role of the distance instructor. Faculty accustomed to conventional teaching methods will have to learn new skills not only to move to a facilitator's role in a learner-centered system, but also learn to utilize the potentials of new telecommunications technologies to facilitate learning and enhance their own effectiveness.

Many faculty remark on changes they make in their teaching both to take advantage of the potential of the technology and to adapt to its limitations when teaching via audioconferencing (Schmidt, Sullivan, and Hardy 1994), audiographics (Gunawardena 1992), computer mediated communication (Boston 1992), and two-way video, one-way audio (Catchpole 1992; Worley 1993). Specific examples of techniques and strategies cited are increased planning and organization of materials and the syllabus, designing instruction to be more learner-centered with students taking an active role in the planning and implementation of activities, and incorporating appropriate mixes of technology such as customized interactive software, pre-produced video, fax, and electronic mail. Dillon and Walsh (1992) found evidence in the research that faculty do alter their roles, although the degree to which this occurs may depend on the technology used, with faculty who use interactive video changing less than those using interactive audio.

Tushnet et al. (1993) note that a number of teachers reported changes in their classroom behavior through participation in the Star Schools activities. In the Massachusetts Corporation for Educational Television (MCET) project teachers had indicated an increase in the use of multiple technologies in the classroom (95%), innovative ways of teaching science (85%), interdisciplinary teaching (71%), cooperative learning (68%), hands-on science (57%), and team teaching (47%). In this project, teachers also reported changes in classroom management strategies, with more emphasis given to organizing classes with small group activities (85% of teachers) and less given to lecturing to the whole class (69%).

In distance education, it is important to think of the role of the instructor in a larger expanded sense. Instructors have to work collaboratively in a team, with tutors, distance learning coordinators, instructional designers, and television production or graphic production personnel.

Thach and Murphy (1994) using a Delphi process identify eleven roles for faculty who teach at a distance. These roles, which might be assumed by one or by several people, include: instructor, instructional designer, technology expert, technician, administrator, site facilitator, support staff, editor, librarian, evaluation specialist, and graphic designer.

A number of studies in the current review would add the roles of collaborator and facilitator to the above list (Boston 1992; Garrison 1993; Schmidt, Sullivan, and Hardy 1994). A common thread among these studies is the view of the instructor as a guide through a shared learning process rather than as an authoritative disseminator of knowledge. This is also how the role of the instructor is viewed in a constructivist approach to instruction, and Garrison (1993) makes it clear that this change in roles does not reduce the instructor to a mere optional resource: "While the focus is on learning and the learner taking responsibility to construct meaning, this does not diminish the role of the teacher...the teacher carries a heavy responsibility to structure content that provides a framework to connect and make sense of ideas and facts. The goal is not simply the assimilation of facts" (p. 203). This is only possible through an instructor who is comfortable assuming many roles, among them those of mediator, modeler, and motivator.

Distance teaching requires faculty to devote much more time to preparation than they would for a face-to-face classroom. In order to encourage faculty to undertake teaching at a distance and make the enterprise attractive to them, faculty must be provided with incentives including financial incentives and other incentives such as adjustments in course load, adequate preparation time, recognition among peers, and credit toward tenure and promotion (Beaudoin 1990; Dillon 1989; Gunawardena 1990). It is also important to provide faculty development programs so that instructors have the necessary support to adapt to a new mode of teaching.

Conclusions and Future Research

This paper has reviewed literature on teaching and learning processes, implications for designing distance instruction, and topics for future research related to five themes: 1) learner-centered instruction, 2) interaction, 3) social presence, 4) cognitive strategies, and 5) collaborative learning. A significant feature that emerged across all five themes is the necessity to change instructor roles in the distance education context. Part of this role change is brought about because of the need to adapt to telecommunications technologies that facilitate the communication process in distance education. Figure 1 illustrates a framework for planning distance instruction based on this review of literature. This figure shows the relationship between teaching and learning processes and changes in faculty roles in the distance education context. Two aspects of the teaching and learning process that require role changes in the distance education environment are designing learner-centered instruction and creating social presence.

The majority of articles and research papers examined in this study are either descriptions of single programs or anecdotal evidence of teaching experience. Very few articles provided empirical evidence on the effectiveness of specific teaching strategies. Future research should examine how specific teaching methods and strategies discussed in this paper impact student achievement and transfer of knowledge. Research should also address how learner characteristics interact with the instructional methods, strategies, and media used in distance classes.

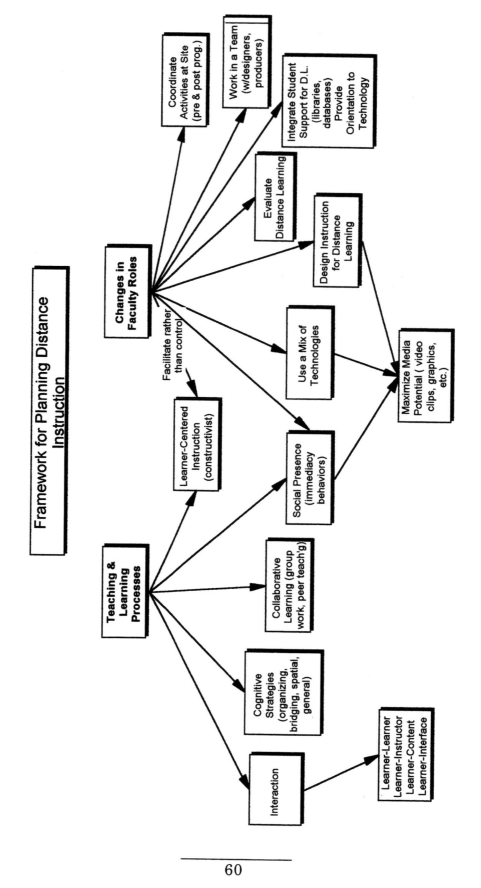

Figure 1. Framework for Planning Distance Instruction

References

Beaudoin, M. 1990. The instructor's changing role in distance education. *The American Journal of Distance Education* 4(2):21–29.

Boston, R. 1992. Remote delivery of instruction via the PC and modem: What have we learned? *The American Journal of Distance Education* 6(3):45–57.

Catchpole, M. J. 1992. Classroom, open, and distance teaching: A faculty view. *The American Journal of Distance Education* 6(3):34–44.

Dede, C. 1989. The evolution of distance learning: Technology-mediated interactive learning. A Report for the Study: Technologies for Learning at a Distance Science Education, and Transportation Program, Office of Technology Assessment, Congress of the United States.

Dillenbourg, P., M. Baker, A. Blaye, and C. O'Malley n.d. The evolution of research on collaborative learning. World Wide Web (WWW) database: http://tecfa.unige.ch. TECFA, University of Geneva, Switzerland.

Dillon, C. L., and S. M. Walsh, 1992. Faculty: The neglected resource in distance education. *The American Journal of Distance Education* 6(3):5–21.

Gagne, R. M., L. J. Briggs, and W. W. Wager. 1988. *Principles of Instructional Design.* (3rd ed.). New York: Holt, Rinehart and Winston.

Garrison, D. R. 1993. A cognitive-constructivist view of distance education: An analysis of teaching-learning assumptions. *Distance Education* 14(2):199–211.

Gunawardena, C. N. 1992. Changing faculty roles for audiographics and online teaching. *The American Journal of Distance Education* 6(3):58–71.

Gunawardena, C. N. 1995. Social presence theory and implications for interaction and collaborative learning in computer conferences. Paper presented at The Fourth International Conference on Computer Assisted Instruction, National Chiao Tung University, Hsinchu, Taiwan, R.O.C.

Hackman, M. Z., and K. B. Walker, 1990. Instructional communication in the televised classroom: The effects of system design and teacher immediacy on student learning and satisfaction. *Communication Education* 39(3):196–209.

Hillman, D. C. A., D. J. Willis, and C. N. Gunawardena. 1994. Learner-interface interaction in distance education: An extension of contemporary models and strategies for practitioners. *The American Journal of Distance Education* 8(2):30–42.

Moore, M. G. 1993. Is teaching like flying? A total systems view of distance education. *The American Journal of Distance Education* 7(1):1–11.

Moore, M. G. 1989. Editorial: Three types of interaction. *The American Journal of Distance Education* 3(2):1–6.

Olgren, C. H. 1992. Adults' learning strategies and outcomes in an independent study course. Ph.D. dissertation, University of Wisconsin-Madison, Madison, WI.

Salomon, G. 1983. Using television as a unique teaching resource for OU courses. (IET Paper No. 225). Milton Keynes, U.K.: The Open University, Institute of Educational Technology.

Schmidt, K. J., M. J. Sullivan, and D. W. Hardy. 1994. Teaching migrant students algebra by audioconference. *The American Journal of Distance Education* 8(3):51–63.

Short, J., E. Williams, and B. Christie. 1976. *The Social Psychology of Telecommunications*. London: John Wiley & Sons.

Thach, L., and K. Murphy. 1994. Collaboration in distance education: From local to international perspectives. *The American Journal of Distance Education* 8(3):5–17.

Tushnet, N., et. al. 1993. Star Schools Evaluation Report One. Los Alamitos, CA: Southwest Regional Laboratory.

Wagner, E. D. 1994. In support of a functional definition of interaction. *The American Journal of Distance Education* 8(2):6–29.

Walther, J. B. 1992. Interpersonal effects in computer-mediated interaction. *Communication Research* 19(1):52–90.

Weir, S., L. Krensky, and S. Gal. 1990. Final Report: Evaluation of the TERC Star Schools Project. Cambridge, MA: TERC, Inc.

Wells, R. A. 1990. Computer-mediated communication for distance education and training: Literature review and international resources. Boise, ID: U. S. Army Research Institute.

West, C. K., J. A. Farmer, and P. M. Wolff. 1991. *Instructional Design: Implications from Cognitive Science.* Englewood Cliffs, NJ: Prentice Hall.

Worley, L. 1993. Educational television and professional development: The Kentucky model. *Technological Horizons in Education* 20(11):70–73.

Note: This paper was supported by the Office of Educational Research and Improvement, U.S. Department of Education, under grant number R203A40026, OSU/NAU Star Schools evaluation.

7 Telecourse-Mediated Staff Development for K-12 Teachers: Review, Update and Implications for Research

Christine S. Jones

On a recent trip, while viewing the petroglyphs of the Anasazi in the canyons of the four corners area of the USA's southwest, I was struck by the implications of these communications which have remained and come to us through the distance of space and time. Although it initially may seem to be a leap of topic and focus, I ask the readers to consider that these artifacts of earlier people's expression have come to and hold our 20th century minds' attention, not unlike the ways in which all media and their subsequent effects and longevity are also the subject of our interests. I therefore begin this paper on my perspectives on research in distance education, past, present and future, with an observation that whatever the media and modes of transmission, the major issues of communication and education still remain: what the message is, transmitted to what audience, in what locale, over what period of time, and for what purpose. Therefore, the issues of quality and medium of instruction still face us and research in distance education must encompass all of these issues.

In particular, my area of research interest has and continues to be distance education in university and K-12 linkages, as these relate specifically to students and their teachers. What follows is a summary of my previous research, my perspectives on the current state of distance education in these arenas and suggestions for future research. Further, to set an agenda for research in distance education, higher education researchers and practitioners must recognize that it is the students who are presently in K-12 classrooms whose needs and usage of distance education will dictate the direction of this agenda. (It is to be noted that while the following research studies focused upon telecourses, I will in no way limit the scope of this paper to this one delivery format. Nor will issues of learning, design, policy, and administration be necessarily excluded because I do not see these areas as mutually exclusive).

In 1989, I conducted a study to analyze and categorize the responses of telecourse students who evaluated the effectiveness of non-interactive telecourses used in graduate education courses at Colorado State University (Jones and Timpson 1991). The research investigated these five variables: 1) the value for graduate education students (who are K-12 teachers) in studying instructional strategies and theories by telecourse; 2) the importance of convenience of telecourses; 3) the value of a collegial experience in viewing the telecourse in a group; 4) the benefits of seeing practicing teachers model various teaching strategies on tape, and the effect of these telecourses on the teacher's confidence and efficacy in their own classrooms.

The sample population of 190 was drawn from over 700 people, primarily professional K-12 teachers enrolled since 1982 in two courses, Advances in Instruction I and II at Colorado State University. Some subjects viewed the telecourses in isolation, and some took the courses at their school site with a cohort group. Three instruments were used for a post-hoc analysis: the standardized final evaluation form used for both on-campus and off-campus delivery of these courses; a follow-up written survey of perceived longer-term telecourse impact; and a follow-up telephone survey. The last two instruments were delivered to a stratified sample of twenty-six and twenty-one subjects, respectively.

The results of this study supported previous research indicating that convenience, access, and an increase in knowledge and skills are important factors for professional educators using distance education. Further, the value of collegiality in site-based staff development has important implications for the professional growth of the faculty unit, both in team building and in improving the work environment and climate. The results of this study suggested that when students (in this case professional educators) worked independently, their self-efficacy improves because of the nature of their isolation. Since the preponderance of distance education is still independent, one might assume that teachers, already isolated, might not benefit from this mode of instruction. However, results of this study also suggested that collegiality can improve when these subjects worked together in on-site study groups.

It was these questions and others which prompted my dissertation research in 1990 (Jones 1991). The purpose of that study was to assess the effectiveness of telecourse mediated site-based staff development of K-12 teachers in impacting school environmental climate and instructional knowledge of critical thinking models, by comparing telecourse delivery to traditional inservice delivery with facilitated and non-facilitated on-site study groups.

This exploratory research studied teachers in two rural Colorado school districts, who were assigned to three treatment groups. Each treatment group received four videotaped modules of a graduate level education course covering four critical thinking teaching models: Induction, Inquiry, Concept Attainment and Synectics (Joyce and Weil 1986). Instruments used were the CFK, Ltd., School Climate Profile (Howard, Howell, and Brainard 1987), questionnaires assessing effects of the treatment, post-test grades for the course, and an analysis of videotapes recorded of the subjects while they worked in the treatment groups.

The results of this research indicated that there was no significant difference among telecourse-facilitated, telecourse non-facilitated, and inservice student groups in their perceptions of school climate factors; the challenge of inservice training was lower than that of a telecourse mediated site-based training model, and teacher subjects in facilitated groups scored higher on assignments than the teacher subjects in the non-facilitated group, while those in the non-facilitated group appeared to be more motivated during the sessions, depended on each other more for the content information and asked each other more questions. In addition to these findings, within the review of literature through 1990, studies assessing the effectiveness of telecourses generally identified instructor feedback, in whatever format (Beare 1989), on-site facilitation (Dillon and Gunawardena 1990), convenience (Bååth 1982), and field dependence or independence (Greene 1987) as important variables concerning student satisfaction and success.

One might argue that the advances in technology over even the last five to six years serve to make the subject and results of this previous research almost as distant in time as the aforementioned petroglyphs. Indeed, since completing these two research projects, over the last five years, my interests and perspectives on these issues have changed only by degree. As a coordinator of programs aimed at improving the science and mathematics content and pedagogy for K-12 teachers, I am acutely involved in seeking ways in which this instructional knowledge and content would be improved. As such, I consider all of this issues regarding the uses of technology for achieving these goals. Whereas, my research focused upon teachers in rural areas, independently or in groups receiving their graduate instruction via telecourses in how to improve instruction, I am now involved in the myriad ways in which teachers and their students might receive both improved content and pedagogy, and I find myself attending endless meetings where the subject of distance education is raised as a potential method to meet these ends.

The context of my work at Colorado State University (CSU) with its history as a leader in distance education has and continues to provide me with ample opportunities to investigate these issues. I trust the reader will indulge a brief review of Colorado State's institutional capabilities, which were instigated in 1967 with the inception of Colorado SURGE (Colorado State University Resources in Graduate Education) to meet the needs of professional engineers.

The program has grown to include all areas of engineering, computer science, and business. In a typical year, ten video classrooms are utilized to deliver over 150 courses. Approximately 1,200 videotapes are shipped to student sites every week. In addition, the College of Business' MBA program is offered to students via direct tape delivery (Switzer and Switzer 1994).

Colorado State was a charter member of National Technological University (NTU) and offers several College of Engineering and Computer Science courses every year on this system. CSU's Office of Instructional Services operates NTU's primary uplink facility on four to twelve digital channels twenty-four hours per day. In addition to credit coursework, CSU and NTU work together to offer an average of fifty live and interactive short courses per year by satellite. The NTU satellite network is the largest all-digital network in operation. Colorado State is a charter member of AG*SAT, which is a satellite consortium of colleges of agriculture cooperating to improve education in agriculture. Pre-produced telecourses in many discipline areas such as education, world languages, and psychology are offered via public television in Denver and Pueblo, as well as over Mind Extension University. A microwave link for the purpose of offering full-motion interactive television capabilities between the University of Wyoming and Colorado State, originates courses at both campuses. Colorado State also holds two-way interactive videoconferences with Adams State College in Alamosa, Colorado and with CSU's Denver Center using compressed video. Colorado State also serves as a central reception site for numerous teleconferences.

Before suggesting subsequent areas for research, it is appropriate to reflect very briefly on the issues of improving teaching and learning that pervade any discussion of these topics, whether the instruction is "live" or at a distance. Ironically, while completing the writing of this paper, I took a break to attend a video teleconference on the subject of improving higher education teaching and learning. Unfortunately and predictably, the interactivity for questions was frustrated by the presumed sheer numbers of calls generated and therefore faxes replaced telephone questions. The medium itself was also questioned by a distant participant who asked the distinguished panel why the audience in the studio and at all of the remote locations were all sitting passively in darkened rooms listening to a panel of talking heads, broadcast over what is touted as an interactive media delivering a message about how to improve teaching and learning by infusing activity and engagement.

The points not to be missed at such an opportunity are that: 1) faculty development at whatever level, higher education and K-12, must itself model effective practice and include intensive follow-up; 2) effective practice means attending to active engagement of learners through a variety of methods including cooperative activities and hands-on work; attending to depth not breadth; attending to and using various learning styles for a variety of learners; and attending to myriad means of evaluating the effectiveness of one's instruction and honoring the learner's feedback; and finally the recognition by administrators at all levels that good teaching is to be valued and rewarded.

In reviewing the scholarly and popular literature of the last five years, the advent of greater accessibility through interactive links, compressed video and the explosion of the information superhighway seems to have added to the urgency of those who want to use distance education, particularly in higher education, K-12 linkages. If the appropriate funds have been located and consortia formed, "hardware" purchased, and courses delivered, then aren't students of every age and school settings in every remote location being served? And what as researchers do we still need to investigate? What follows is a description of some of the specific delivery systems and projects discovered in this most recent literature, and the questions for research which each of these has generated in my mind. A clarification: I do not see these as barriers, necessarily, to quality distance education. Rather these questions have arisen when I consider the previous discussion of quality instruction and learning.

An extremely useful addition to the distance education resource conversation is the National Distance Learning Center (NDLC) Database System, accessible in the nineties' newest arena, cyberspace. In its own language, the NDLC has "no vested interest in promoting any particular provider's programming or materials and gives all providers equal billing and is equally accessible to potential users and facilitators." At this writing, the database claimed 14,000 individual listings with 50-100 new listings added each week, with users in all fifty states and U.S. territories. Surely, the researcher seeking to assess the effectiveness of various distance education opportunities may now travel the NDLC's on ramp to find programming ready for evaluation. The questions of quality, however, still remain with no presumption on the part of this information service to judge this attribute. Nor would it be easier to directly involve the targeted populations for these assessments, since the larger and more diffuse audiences for these services and the means by which users access the information and potentially the programming also continues to broaden.

In *Education Week* (West 1995a), Linda Roberts, a special adviser on education to U.S. Secretary of Education Richard Riley, notes that in several recent national surveys, respondents gave the highest possible ratings to the idea that the information superhighway should carry interactive television programs. "This is phenomenal." says Roberts. "It says to me that the public as a whole has really got it right. The information superhighway has the potential to bring the best of the world to our classrooms" (p. 6). However, this eagerness and the aforementioned urgency is also accompanied by a high anxiety over how to use these technologies. This anxiety translates in the need for widespread on-going training of faculty K-16 in the use of these technologies, i.e., the "net," as well as all of the previously labeled "audio-visual" equipment for enhancement, projection, and enrichment of instruction.

Important issues arise over governance and costs of providing the latest in computers as well as the large expense of converting existing transmission media to the latest in faster, high volume transmission media. Federal Communications Commission Chair Reed Hundt (West 1995b), as well as in a follow-up commentary (Hundt 1995), states that from their individual classrooms, teachers must be able to send and receive faxes, upload and download information from communications satellites, have access to interactive television programming, communicate with parents at home over telephone lines, and join the virtual communities of their colleagues online. He says, "We need everybody concerned, especially the parents to . . . say yes, my kid is being deprived every day of the chance to participate in the communications revolution" (p. 7).

Beyond wiring, infrastructure, and the latest incarnations of computers, the question remains who is providing the transmissions of courses, tapes, videodisks, CD-ROMs, and/or multi-media packages of content. Studios in institutions of higher education, school districts, private not for profit, and private for profit companies all compete in the provider market. Whether the product is a taped SURGE class from Colorado State, a small-scale science class broadcast from the central studio in the Poudre R-1 school district in Colorado to a junior high classroom, cable programs broadcast into elementary classrooms using the TCI network, taped science videos purchased from INSIGHTS or NASA footage of a space shuttle mission broadcast over digital lines through the EduPort to high school students in Nebraska, the responsibility for designing and producing the product rests with the producers and the responsibility for using the product rests with the teacher in the classroom.

The earlier mentioned good practices of instruction must be manifest by both sender and receiver. The live, taped, or otherwise packaged transmission must engage the learner, attend to the different learning modalities (visual, auditory and kinesthetic), provide for learner exploration and extension of the content, and suggest ways in which the learning may be evaluated. A lecture or a panel discussion, with the addition of perhaps a quicktime movie, may not meet these criteria for good practice. On the receiving end, the teacher or facilitator must prepare the students for this transmission with attention to an engaging introduction to the learning; attention to the setting, lights, and room arrangement; opportunities for interaction among the learners; attention to time to process and clarify the understanding of the information of the transmission; attention to the learners' questions; attention to the learner's applications and extensions of the materials; and effective closure to the transmission.

This may be a tall order. However, I submit that even if all of the "hardware" is paid for and in place and operational, these instructional issues must still be at the core of distance education. Recognizing that the following are by no means the only collaborative K-12 projects worthy of investigation, researchers would seem to have a rich arena to investigate these questions within the California projects. The California State University (CSU) systems' program DELTA funds both inter- and intracampus projects such as the Distributed Learning Resources project to transmit applications of CSU Hayward's tunneling electron microscope across the state. San Jose State University is planning to deliver two-way video courses in library science and other disciplines, which may not have a critical mass at any one campus, from CSU-San Francisco over Pacific Bell's ATM network. Pacific Bell's California Research and Education Network (CalREN) has also recently funded two year's worth of advance networking services for forty-eight education projects. A project through the University of California Berkeley is the Electronic Mentoring, Teaching, and Information Resource Network which targets disadvantaged students in urban and rural areas. Connected to a dozen university departments with numerous minority community and high school partners, this network will develop curricula to connect students of all ages to use university resources and the World Wide Web. The Lawrence Hall of Science at Berkeley is preparing a tour of the human brain over the network.

Questions still remain. What happens when the funding sources "dry up"? Will this "hardware" go the way of the petroglyphs by the time it is implemented? More specifically, will learners have across-the-board access to all of these technologies: both rural learners, who have fewer funding sources and are located far from universities, and urban learners, who currently are the targets of increased funding? Currently, the access is spotty and uneven within school buildings, and computers and telecommunications equipment may be behind locked doors, available only to those limited number of learners targeted by a small specific project. And who is responsible for the quality of the message? Lanham suggests that the convergence of social, technological, and theoretical factors tells us both what our traditional essence is, and how we might express it in practices that will give our students a framework appropriate for our times. (Lanham 1993). Researchers will be busy through the millennium and beyond.

References

Bååth, J. A. 1982. Empirical findings and theoretical deliberations. *Distance Education* 3:6–27.

Beare, P. L. 1989. The comparative effectiveness of videotape, audiotape, and telelecture in delivering continuing education teacher education. *The American Journal of Distance Education* 3(2):57–66.

Dillon, C. L., and C. Gunawardena. 1990. Learner support as the critical link in distance education: A study of the Oklahoma television instructional system. Norman, OK: University of Oklahoma, Oklahoma Research Center for Continuing Professional and Higher Education.

Greene, J. C. 1987. The effects of small group and instructor led discussions in the academic achievement of field-dependent community college telecourse students. Unpublished doctoral dissertation. Michigan State University, East Lansing, Michigan.

Howard, E. R., B. Howell, and E. Brainard. 1987. *Handbook for Conducting School Climate Improvement Projects.* Bloomington, IN: The Phi Delta Kappa Educational Foundation.

Hundt, R. E. 1995. Bring the revolution home. *Education Week* 14(32):52.

Jones, C., and W. Timpson. 1991. Technologically mediated staff development: A retrospective case study. *The American Journal of Distance Education* 5(1):51–56.

Jones, C. 1991. Telecourse mediated site-based staff development among general and vocational educators. Unpublished doctoral dissertation. Colorado State University, Fort Collins, Colorado.

Joyce, B., and M. Weil. 1986. *Models of Teaching.* Englewood Cliffs, NJ: Prentice-Hall.

Lanham, R. A. 1993. *The Electronic Word: Democracy, Technology and the Arts.* Chicago, IL: The University of Chicago Press.

Switzer, J. S., and R. V. Switzer. 1994. Copyright question: Using audiovisual works in a satellite-delivered program. *T.H.E. Journal* 21(5):76–79.

West, P. 1995a. Wired for the future. *Education Week* 14(16):3–9.

West, P. 1995b. Paving the way for the highway. *Education Week* 14(16):7.

<table>
<tr><td>8</td><td>**Library Support for Quality in Distance Education: A Research Agenda**

Marie A. Kascus</td></tr>
</table>

Introduction

Insuring quality in distance education is the collaborative responsibility of all constituents in the educational process: institutions, accrediting bodies, faculty, and libraries. Institutions have a responsibility to provide the resources and oversight to insure quality instruction and comparable degrees making certain that students use these resources as an integral part of the educational process. Regional accrediting bodies have a responsibility to provide standards that maintain quality without stifling creativity and to apply them uniformly to the extended campus. Faculty have a responsibility to design and deliver courses that are equivalent to those offered on campus and, when relevant, to include a library research component to encourage independent learning. The library community has a responsibility to provide standards for extended campus library service and to educate librarians to help distant learners become information literate. As more emphasis is placed on institutions without walls, research from all constituents is needed to objectively document how well each contributes to improving the quality of distance education.

Library support is central to the design, delivery, organization, and administration of quality distance education programs. In a recent survey of library school deans and directors, half of the respondents agreed with the statement that the lack of library support is perceived by off-campus students and faculty as a disadvantage of off-campus instructional programs (Kascus 1994a). If there is a perception that distance education courses are taught differently because of the lack of library support, research is needed to test that perception. However, in the current electronic age, access to library and learning resources at a distance is entirely feasible. Remote access technology is helping to bridge the gap between the library and the distant learner and has the potential to significantly enhance the quality of distance education.

The literature of extended campus and distance education librarianship will be examined to assess what research has been done and what research needs to be done to effectively meet the library and information needs of distant learners and the faculty who teach them.

Historical Background

One of the generally accepted rationales for off-campus and distance education programs is to increase access to higher education for those geographically isolated. Ironically, the implications of such development for the provision of library support were largely overlooked in early pioneering efforts. Some institutions opted to ignore the problem of providing library support rather than to confront it head on. Distant learners were left to fend for themselves in satisfying their library and information needs or totally spoon-fed in an effort to compensate for the logistical problems posed in providing service at a distance.

With the proliferation of off-campus and distance education programs, regional accrediting bodies raised concerns about quality. In the process, they strengthened their resolve about the importance of library support for those programs modifying the language of the standards to recognize access as a way of supplementing ownership. Faculty were expected to make library research assignments appropriate to the level of the course to help students develop their intellectual skills. Institutions were expected to remind faculty of the importance of the library to course outcomes. With time and the creative efforts of a group of off-campus librarians, some institutions developed model programs of service finding new and innovative ways to meet the special needs of the off-campus population.

The early efforts of librarians in distance library service were directed at meeting the immediate need for support where none was planned. Early library support is best characterized by the idea of "fetch and deliver" which left the distant learner little opportunity to experience the full range of library resources or to develop library research skills (Cullen 1994). With time, the concern became one of providing services equal to what was provided for on-campus students. These efforts were initially directed at providing a comparable student experience by traditional means such as journal acquisition, photocopying services, adjusting circulation loan periods, collection development, document delivery, extending library hours, and interlibrary loan. Later, innovative services were developed such as toll-free telephone reference and literature search request, on–site bibliographic instruction, facsimile delivery, and cooperative arrangements with other libraries to provide services either through informal verbal agreements or through formal written contract. Marketing became an effective strategy for off-campus librarians in making faculty and students aware of available services.

Telecommunications technology is fueling the next stage of development in library support at a distance with a vision of the virtual library providing access to the full resources of the library and more. With the assimilation of technology into every aspect of library service, the potential for providing quality support for distance education is greatly enhanced. Remote access technology is bridging the gap between the library and the distant learner. The online catalog of the home library, as well as catalogs of other libraries near and far, are available through dial-up access. Also available are CD-ROM subject databases for searching via dial-up access or local area networks. Electronic mail can be used for reference and information request service. Electronic journals are adding a new dimension to scholarly communication for faculty and students. New information sources not owned by any library are accumulating almost daily and are accessible on the Internet. The potential for electronic access and delivery of library and information resources, according to Bruffee, has the potential to turn distance learning into the equivalent of a "real" college and university education if the distance learning program revises its understanding of what learning is and what libraries are (Bruffee 1993).

Now there is both a need and an opportunity for librarians to look at library and information services more globally. The blurring of institutional boundaries and library walls is making it necessary for libraries to look at their services and value added services as an aspect of that service. Some of the most creative possibilities in library support are happening in the overlap with remote communications technology. Remote access technology is the link between traditional and non-traditional library service bringing the two together for the long term benefit of distance education. New and evolving technology is making it possible to go well beyond what has previously been possible in supporting the growing population of distant learners and remote users.

Literature on Library Support for Distant Learners: Content, Change, Trends

Despite the long history of extension service, it was not until 1931 that the American Library Association first recognized that extension students were at a disadvantage because of the lack of library resources for this constituency (ALA 1931). In the period 1930 to 1970, very little was written on the topic in library literature. Since that time, the body of literature on library support for the distant learner has grown considerably. The first growth span coincided with the establishment of open universities in several countries in the 1970s contributing forty publications, and the second growth span coincided with the growth of distance education programs in traditional post secondary institutions in the 1980s contributing 361 publications. (Latham, Slade, and Budnick 1991).

In the first comprehensive bibliography on the topic of library services for off-campus and distance education published in 1991, 535 works were listed under fourteen broad categories: bibliographies, general works, historical studies, role of libraries in distance education, guidelines and standards, organization and planning, collection management, information and support services, bibliographic instruction, document delivery, interlibrary cooperation, library surveys, user studies, and library case studies (Latham, Slade, and Budnick 1991). A second volume of this bibliography is in progress and lists (518) works using the same fourteen categories with the addition of the category "remote access to electronic resources." The 1991 bibliography covered the sixty year period between 1930 and 1990. The second volume of this bibliography continues the coverage from 1991 to 1994. It also lists earlier publications omitted in the original bibliography, revisions of earlier entries, and a few publications with a 1995 imprint. The literature included in the forthcoming second volume provides the focus of the following discussion.

The published bibliography and the forthcoming second volume are intended to be comprehensive in their coverage of the publication productivity in the area of library services for off-campus and distance education. For that reason, they include citations to a wide range of sources including conference proceedings, newsletters, pamphlets, unpublished reports, chapters in monographs, masters and doctoral theses, and journal articles. Conference proceedings from the Fifth (New Mexico) and Sixth (St. Louis) Off-Campus Library Services Conferences sponsored by Central Michigan University account for seventy of the publications in the forthcoming bibliography. Special issues of *Library Trends* and *Illinois Libraries* on the topic account for thirty-five publications. In addition to these two topical issues, journal and newsletter articles account for another 193 publications. Theses accounted for sixteen of the references, and chapters in monographs accounted for thirty-nine publications.

The literature represents a broad international focus with representation from thirty-three countries and geographic areas. The United States accounted for 231 publications, Australia ninety-nine, India fifty-three, United Kingdom fifty, Canada thirty, and South Africa nineteen. Other countries and geographic areas represented include Antigua, Caribbean, Finland, Ghana, Greece, Grenada, Guyana, Jamaica, Kenya, Netherlands, New Zealand, Nigeria, Singapore, South Pacific Region, Spain, Sri Lanka, Taiwan, Tanzania, Thailand, and Zambia. There is a marked increase in publication activity in developing countries such as India where illiteracy is a national problem and distance education a potential solution.

The majority of the publications listed in each of the major categories describe practice and application rather than report research findings. Three of the major categories represent the principal research methodologies that have been used: user studies, library case studies, and library surveys. Selected research studies in these categories will be discussed along with studies from "general works" and "remote access to electronic resources" to provide some insight into content, change, and trends in reporting research findings. While the number of actual research studies is small in comparison to the total publication output, they are important to advancing the field of distance learning because they provide measurable information about what is good practice and what can be done to improve practice. Some good work is being done, but there is much more that needs to be done to provide a solid research base.

User Studies. User studies are library statistical surveys that involve carefully planned questionnaires or interviews designed to evaluate user satisfaction or dissatisfaction. User studies are important in identifying problems and issues faced by distant learners in accessing library and learning resources. Such studies provide the basis for continuous improvement in library service and need to be conducted regularly. Of the forty-four contributions in this category, twelve are from the United States, six are from the United Kingdom, five are from Canada, fourteen are from Australia, and seven other. Unwin (1994) surveyed 350 postgraduate distance learning students and found that while students recognize the importance of the library for their development, they experience many difficulties in accessing library services. The author stresses the need for a systematic review of how library resources can be integrated into distance education programs. Craig and Schultz (1993) investigated MSA graduate students' perceptions of the effectiveness of library instruction to the successful completion of assignments in courses and the final integration process at Central Michigan University (CMU). Survey results indicate that library instruction was effective in helping students understand the research process and better utilize CMU's library services. Burge and Howard (1990) surveyed graduate students at the Ontario Institute for Studies in Education and found that 29% reported that access to library resources was excellent while 68% rated it fair. They suggest that the improvement of library services is partly dependent on enhanced access and partly a function of building the need for library resources into course design. Behrens (1992) investigated the role of library skills in first year undergraduate courses at the University of South Africa using a typology of research skills. Results of the study indicate that library skills are a prototype of information gathering strategies relevant to the lifelong learning aspect of information literacy. The importance of independent information seeking for students and librarian/faculty partnerships to teach library skills across the curriculum are recommended.

Research findings from user studies tell us that students recognize the importance of libraries to their academic success, that they have difficulties in accessing library resources at a distance, and that they do not regularly use the library. These studies tell us that faculty profess the importance of library use but that their class assignments do not reflect this. The studies indicate that library instruction contributes to student effectiveness in course assignments and that library skills contribute to lifelong learning. Perhaps more needs to be done to encourage faculty to design courses that include a library module. It may also be necessary for librarians to do a better job of promoting library services to increase faculty and student awareness of the services that are available to them.

Library Surveys. Library surveys organize, present, and summarize data. Library surveys are a useful tool in collecting measurable information for comparative study. Of the twenty-six contributions in this category, ten were from the United States, six from the United Kingdom, three from Australia, two from Canada, two from India, and three were international in scope. Slade (1994) reports the findings of an inter-university survey of distance learner's library use and satisfaction with the services provided by six universities in western Canada. Fifteen students from each institution were interviewed over the telephone. While most students were satisfied with the services received, a need for more library instruction was indicated. Van Blair (1989) reports on research to determine the funding methods used to provide library services to off-campus students and faculty. Four funding models were identified: larger general library budget, library fee for off-campus students, a percentage of the off-campus tuition budget, and bargaining for funding with off-campus administrators. Corrigan (1993) investigates the coordinating mechanisms between extended degree programs and off-campus library services. Survey results of sixty-eight of 104 institutions responding indicate that off-campus program administrators perceive a moderate frequency of discussion with librarians, no formal responsibilities for library services, a moderate degree of influence over decisions about library services, and a moderate match between program mission and the manner in which library support was provided.

Case Studies. Case studies of individual libraries are a good source of institutional data and provide working models and useful ideas for other libraries planning library support for off-campus and distance education programs. Of the seventy-seven contributions included in this category, forty-two are from the United States, ten from Australia, four from Canada, two from the United Kingdom, and nineteen others represent South Africa, Taiwan, India, Caribbean, Spain, and New Zealand. Burge and Snow (1990) describe principles for effective practice in interactive audio classrooms reflecting the learner-centered view adopted at Ontario Institute for Studies in Education. Library issues include collaborative relationships between librarians and distance students in meeting students' information needs and regular communication between librarians and distance educators. Fisher uses the University of Birmingham, England to discuss measuring the effectiveness of a distance learning program. The process includes measuring library usage, tabulating library costs, comparing costs with those of similar libraries, measuring educational effectiveness, and measuring overall effectiveness.

Elements in the process have relevance for other institutions. Hoy and Hale (1991) compared references cited by on-campus and off-campus graduate library science students at Emporia State University. While the emphasis is on establishing a methodology, results from the study indicate that off-campus students appear not to be disadvantaged in gaining access to scholarly work.

General Works. This category includes publications of a broader focus that do not fall comfortably under the other fourteen major categories. Kascus (1994a) conducted a survey of all schools of library and information science in the United States and Canada to investigate how well the topic of support for off-campus and distance education programs is represented in the curriculum of Library and Information Science (LIS). Findings from the survey provide baseline data on the current level of commitment of LIS curriculum to the topic of library support for off-campus and distance education programs. The findings indicate that the topic is minimally represented in the curriculum and of low priority for most library school deans and directors. As Guest Editor of the *Journal of Education for Library and Information Science,* Kascus (1994b) raised the topic as a library education issue that schools of library and information science need to consider with regard to educating LIS students.

Remote Access Technology and the Distant Learner. This category has been added to the fourteen categories in the 1991 bibliography reflecting a new area of interest for off-campus and distance education librarians. The publications in this category are further divided into those that discuss the topic in a general way and those that refer specifically to the distant learner. Of the seventy-seven publications in this category, fifty-one are general in nature and twenty-six specifically address remote access to electronic sources for the distant learner. In the general category, Billings et al. (1994) implemented and tested a prototype solution to providing remote reference assistance for users who are accessing networked information resources at remote locations. Librarians are able to assist users in real-time by remote intervention in the online search process. Kalin (1991) studied the searching behavior of remote users of Penn State's online catalog comparing the searches to those of in-house users. Remote users were found to be more proficient in terms of their conceptual knowledge, but had more difficulty with procedural details in how to use the online catalog. The searching behavior of remote users has implications for public service librarians in terms of providing appropriate support services. Cutright (1993) describes a successful grant funded demonstration of remote access to CD-ROM, rapid response to information requests, and document delivery specifically for the distant learner. A seminar is used to instruct distant learners on how to access the network system. Interlibrary loan requests are available on the system and facilitate document delivery.

With remote access technology the library has come full circle from the early image of spoon-feeding distant learners to the current vision of empowering distant learners to become information literate and self-directed learners. Remote access can be provided to library catalogs, CD-ROM databases, electronic mail, bulletin boards, and the Internet. The virtual library is changing the distance learning paradigm. One of the important advantages of remote access technology for distance education is the ability to search large numbers of databases simultaneously which greatly facilitates interdisciplinary trespass and collaborative learning. Much more responsibility is placed on distant learners in terms of research and document delivery which contributes to them taking charge of this aspect of their learning. In this category, technology is bridging the gap between traditional library services and extended campus library services with remote access being the common concern. What is of particular interest here is that these publications represent the intersection of the literature on traditional library service and extended campus library service. For that reason, there will most likely be a marked increase in research activity in relation to remote access benefiting distance learning and librarianship.

Concluding Remarks

From the above discussion, there is much to be optimistic about in terms of growth of the literature on library support for the distant learner and the beginnings of research. However, what is evident from reviewing the body of literature as a whole is an imbalance between the abundance of descriptions of the intricacies of practice and the sparsity of empirical research studies that are important for the recognition and further development of distance librarianship as an emerging knowledge base.

While the body of literature is growing at a rapid pace, it remains largely descriptive and non-analytic as is true of much of the literature of distance education itself. What progress has been made has come from the field and what is missing is a basic theory and a broad understanding that contributes to refining practice and fostering new applications. Much of the publication productivity in this area has been reported outside of the conventional library milieu with much of it appearing in conference proceedings, working papers, research reports, and would benefit from being brought into the mainstream of library literature through the refereed publication process for discussion by a wider audience.

The lack of a strong research base weakens distance librarianship and makes it difficult to reach consensus on the essential criteria to use in documenting good practice and measuring performance. Practice and theory have to be brought into alignment so that they inform, enrich, and stimulate each other. While studies of practice are important to a shared understanding, more research needs to be done to establish generally accepted principles that can guide future progress in improving library services for distance learning students and faculty. Comparative and evaluative research data need to be collected and empirical studies conducted that document successful outcomes of library support for distant learners. This will help strengthen the credibility of distance education as a viable alternative to classroom education in the minds of those that are not already convinced.

In looking to the future of library support for the distant learner, what seems most appropriate at this point is a greater emphasis on developing an analytic perspective that can be used to make broad generalizations about improving practice. The research focus needs to be on: 1) establishing evaluative criteria that can be used to measure performance, 2) collecting data and testing assumptions through carefully planned research, and 3) using the results of that research to forge a common methodology that is valid across institutions.

References

ALA books for the Extension Student. 1931. *ALA Bulletin* 30:674–687.

Behrens, S. J. 1992. Undergraduate library and information skills in a distance learning environment. D. Bibl. thesis, University of South Africa, Pretoria, Transvaal, South Africa.

Billings, H., I. E. Carver, J. D. Racine, and J. Tongate. 1994. Remote reference assistance for electronic information resources over networked workstations. *Library Hi Tech* 12(1) consecutive issue 45:77–86.

Bruffee, K. A. 1993. Mime and supermime: Collaborative learning and instructional technology. In *Collaborative Learning: Higher Education, Interdependence, and the Authority of Knowledge,* 98–110. Baltimore: Johns Hopkins University Press.

Burge, E. J., and J. Howard. 1990. Graduate level distance learning: The students speak. *Canadian Journal of University Continuing Education* 16(1):49–65.

Burge, E. J. and J. E. Snow. 1990. Interactive audio classrooms: Key principles for "effective practice." *Education for Information* 8:299–312.

Corrigan, A. C. 1993. A study of coordinating mechanisms between external degree programs and off-campus library services as perceived by external degree program administrators. Ed.D. diss., West Virginia University, Morgantown, West Virginia.

Craig, M. H., and K. E. Schultz. 1993. Off-campus students' perceptions of the effectiveness of library user education. In *The Sixth Off-Campus Library Services Conference Proceedings,* comp. C. J. Jacob, 73–77. Mount Pleasant, MI: Central Michigan University.

Cullen, S. 1994. Changes and challenges in information skills for off-campus and open learning students. In *Access Through Open Learning: With a Major Focus on Achieving Flexibility,* eds. A. Ellis and J. Lowe, 195–198. Lismore, NSW: Norsearch.

Cutright, P. J. 1993. Applying innovative technology to the needs of the distant learner. *Library Hi Tech* 11(4):67–74.

Fisher, R. K. 1991. Measuring the effectiveness of an off-campus library programme: A case study at the University of Birmingham, England. In *The Fifth Off-Campus Library Services Conference Proceedings,* comp. C. J. Jacob, 93–100. Mount Pleasant, MI: Central Michigan University.

Hoy, C., and M. L. Hale. 1991. A comparison of references cited by on-campus and off-campus graduate library science students. In *The Fifth Off-Campus Library Services Conference Proceedings,* comp. C. J. Jacob, 123–130. Mount Pleasant, MI: Central Michigan University.

Kalin, S. W. 1991. The searching behavior of remote users: A study of one online public access catalog (OPAC). In *ASIS '91: Proceedings of the 54th ASIS (American Society for Information Science) Annual Meeting,* ed. J. Griffiths, 78–185. Medford, NJ: Learned Information.

Kascus, M. A. 1994a What library schools teach about library support to distant students: A survey. *The American Journal of Distance Education* 8(1):20–35.

Kascus, M. A. 1994b. Library support to distant students as a library education and continuing education issue. *Journal of Education for Library and Information Science* 35(4):344–347.

Latham, S., A. Slade, and C. Budnick. 1991. *Library Services for Off-Campus and Distance Education: An Annotated Bibliography.* Canadian Library Association, Library Association Publishing, American Library Association.

Slade, A. L. 1994. Inter-university library survey of off-campus students in western Canada: Summary of results. The D.ED. Letter: Newsletter of the Distance Education Interest Group of the Canadian Library Association 5(1):D1–D28.

Unwin, L. 1994. I'm a real student now: The importance of library access for distance learning students. *Journal of Further and Higher Education* 18(1):85–91.

Van Blair, B. A. 1989. Determining effective methods of funding library services in support of off-campus programs. Ed.D. diss., University of Arkansas, Fayetteville, Arkansas.

Appendix

Priority Topics that Might Contribute to Improvement in Quality in Distance Education

- Studies that compare the attitudes and performance of off-campus students with their on campus counterparts in relation to learning support services such as the library (Analysis of citations in bibliographies documenting research papers for on- and off-campus students)

- Studies that measure library learning outcomes in terms of the success of students in becoming information literate and self-directed learners (As part of a student "capstone" experience, have students develop portfolios of their work, according to a pre-established set of criteria, that demonstrate knowledge, competencies, and skills. Included here could be such things as well documented research papers, exhaustive annotated bibliographies on a particular topic, etc. This would provide both the library and the academic department with relevant assessment data.)

- Studies that measure the effectiveness of incorporating library and information skills into the curriculum (Faculty/librarian collaboration in developing course syllabi, reading lists, reserve lists, and library instruction)

- Studies that investigate how remote access to electronic resources is contributing to quality in distance learning (Measure the attitudes and perceptions of faculty and students to the value added services available through the online catalog, through gateways, enhancements, and seamless access.)

- Studies that evaluate library service from faculty/student perspective (Student diaries recording experiences in using the library through courses and final classroom projects)

<table>
<tr><td>9</td><td>

The Nature and Value of Interaction in Distance Learning

Greg Kearsley

</td></tr>
</table>

One of the most important instructional elements of contemporary distance education is interaction. It is widely held that a high level of interaction is desirable and positively affects the effectiveness of any distance education course. However, it is not clear from research or evaluation data that interaction does improve the quality of learning in most distance education programs. Furthermore, there is little attention to the cost/benefits of interaction in terms of preparation time versus instructional effects.

This article examines the theoretical and empirical basis for interactivity in distance education in the specific context of the Educational Technology Leadership program which is offered through Mind Extension University using a combination of instructional television and a computer bulletin board system.

What is Interactivity?

Interactivity is a complex variable that has many different facets. In terms of "classic" instructional theory, the significance of interaction is that it provides the means for learners to receive feedback (see Dempsey and Sales 1994). In so far as feedback determines successful learning progress (through correction of mistakes or motivation), it can be argued that the more interaction provided, the better. In the context of traditional classroom teaching, Flanders (1970) made detailed studies of student-teacher interaction and concluded that increased interaction improved student achievement and attitudes towards learning.

Moore (1989) identified three types of interaction: student-content, student-teacher, and student-student. This fundamental distinction provides a basis for analyzing the relative significance of different types of interaction in a distance education program. Each type of interaction could have different effects on learners or the effectiveness of a course. In traditional classroom instruction, the focus has been on student-teacher interaction. On the other hand, in the development of self-study materials (especially computer-based), the focus has been on student-content interaction. Until recent interest in collaborative/cooperative learning and the use of computer networks, little attention was devoted to student-student interaction.

A further distinction needs to be made between immediate ("real-time") and delayed ("asynchronous") interaction. In traditional classroom teaching, student-teacher interaction is normally immediate. However, in distance education, interaction can be immediate with some media (e.g., teleconferences) or delayed with others (e.g., correspondence or computer networks). This distinction between delayed or immediate interaction is very significant because it determines the logistics and "feel" of the distance learning experience. In order to have immediate interaction, students must participate at a fixed time whereas with delayed interaction, participation is according to the student's schedule. So, distance education programs that involve delayed interaction provide more student control and flexibility. On the other hand, classes that involve immediate interaction often have a sense of excitement and spontaneity that is not present with delayed interaction.

Finally, it is important to note that individuals appear to differ in their propensity for interaction depending upon their personality, age, and/or cognitive and learning styles. Students who are more self-directed or autonomous may want or need less interaction than others. In general, professionals and executives tend to prefer less interactivity, whereas young children tend to want a high level of interaction. So the effectiveness of interaction may vary across individuals or groups.

In summary, the concept of interaction, as it applies to distance learning, is more complicated than it has been treated in traditional instructional theory or classroom teaching. Interaction in distance learning needs to be differentiated according to content versus teacher versus student, immediate versus delayed, and types of learners.

Forms of Interaction

The nature of interaction also varies with the type of media or delivery system used: written (typed), audio (voice), video (face-to-face), or tactile (response units). The classic form of interaction for correspondence study was written assignments and feedback; this still represents the main form of communication between student and teacher/tutor in most open university and independent study courses, although correspondence may now be sent by fax which dramatically speeds up the turnaround time. Computer-mediated communication also represents a form of written interaction. However, while the communication is in typed form, the interaction is much more complex than traditional writing since messages can have many characteristics (e.g., public versus private, forwarding, file attachments) and can also be searched, edited, and/or filed. Furthermore, a different style of written communication is required for network communication compared to traditional correspondence (see e.g., Angell and Heslop 1994).

Audio interaction is usually via a telephone or microphone. In the context of an audioconference, the instructor must structure and manage the discourse very skillfully in order to produce effective classes since otherwise there is a high potential for confusion, chaos, or boredom. On the other hand, there is typically little, if any, preparation for the audio portion of a teleconference since this is primarily used to answer questions from the audience. The sound quality of audio interaction is always a consideration in audio teleconferences; poor quality may significantly reduce the effectiveness of a program.

Video interaction is a relatively new phenomenon since two-way videoconferencing systems are just beginning to be commonly used. Clearly the quality of the transmission, determined by the transmission speed and frame rate, affects how people interact via video. Presumably other characteristics of the conferencing environment, such as lighting, acoustics, room and seat layout, and decor, also affect interaction. Their impact is unknown at the present time.

Tactile interaction has not been widely explored, except in the context of student response units used with television classes. With these devices students are able to respond on a keypad to questions posed by the instructor, who sees an immediate display of the responses on a computer screen. While this provides for a very limited form of interaction, it does provide a means for surveying all students at the same time (the equivalent of asking people to raise their hands in a traditional classroom). Other possible forms of tactile interaction include the use of a lightpen or mouse to draw or annotate in an audiographics system, the use of a joystick in a computer simulation or game to make selections, and the use of body motion sensors in a virtual reality system.

While we know a little about each of these different forms of interaction in the context of their most common usage, we do not know much about mixing and combining different modes of interaction. This is becoming an important issue in the age of multimedia systems which allow written, audio, video, and tactile interaction.

Empirical Studies

While there are many studies that have investigated the effects of interactivity, few of these studies truly isolate the interactive component from other aspects of the distance learning activity, nor do they distinguish the different facets of interaction discussed above. It is not surprising, therefore, that the results of these studies are inconsistent and equivocal.

Some early studies of correspondence programs (e.g., Ahlm 1972; Beijer 1972) looked at the effects of adding telephone interaction with a tutor to courses. These studies indicated that the addition of the tutor made little difference in student achievement and that only a small proportion of students actually used the tutor. Of course, the nature and quality of the interaction provided by tutors could affect this finding. For example, Rekkedal (1983) showed that the effectiveness of correspondence study was improved when feedback from tutors was provided in a more timely manner (see also Rifkind 1992).

A popular issue has been the relative merits of "live" television (one-way television with two-way audio interaction) versus use of videotapes of the same classes without the interactive capability. Barker (1986) reports on a high school Spanish program delivered by live satellite television the first year and then in videotaped form the second year. Barker reports that the taped version without the capability for interaction was less effective. On the other hand, Speth, Poggio, and Glassnapp (1991) did not find interaction to be a significant aspect of achievement in a satellite-delivered foreign language class. Similarly, Stone (1988) in assessing the value of interactive television versus videotapes in the context of graduate engineering, concludes that the interactivity did not make a significant difference.

The use of computer mediated conferencing for student and teacher interaction seems to have produced generally positive results (e.g., Harasim 1990; Waggoner 1992). While there are few quantitative analyses, student and teacher anecdotes indicate that computer networks allow a high degree of interaction among students and instructors. On the other hand, students and teachers sometimes report that the use of computers can be frustrating and introduce a lot of complexity to a course.

An issue of current interest is the relative merits of one-way video with two-way audio versus full two-way video. Studies have shown that the two-way video is more effective than the television plus audio format (e.g., Massoumian

1989). Studies do not show if this is due to the capability for visual rather than audio feedback, the capability to respond more easily, or some other characteristic of videoconferences.

Research Issues

As the brief survey of research above illustrates, existing studies do not really address the following fundamental questions relating to interactivity:

- Is frequency of interaction in a course a meaningful measure?
- Is interaction more important for certain groups of learners than others (e.g., children vs adults)?
- Is interaction more critical in certain kinds of learning than others?
- Does interaction affect learning outcomes such as retention or transfer?
- Does interaction increase student comprehension/understanding?
- Does interactivity always improve learner satisfaction?
- What form of interaction is the most critical?
- Does or should the pattern of interaction change over a course/program?

In order to examine these issues, we need studies that isolate specific dimensions of interaction. We also need descriptive studies that provide a clear picture of interactivity as it currently exists in distance education courses. A recent doctoral study completed by one of our graduate students (Nichol 1994) illustrates this latter category. Nichol collected videotapes of live television classes from a number of different distance education institutions and developed a rating system to classify the kind of interactions present in the classes as well as the nature of the teaching/learning activities. Nichol found that interaction between student and instructor was much more common than interaction among students, content, or equipment. He also found that the amount of interaction increased as the complexity of learning increased, i.e., there was more interaction at an application level than memory tasks. One of the interesting questions raised by this study is the extent to which the results would be the same for a different delivery system (e.g., audioconferencing or computer networks).

Creating Interaction

Even though there are many unanswered questions about interactivity, it is still possible to provide guidelines for improving the degree of interactivity in distance education. A variety of techniques for creating learner participation and generating discussions are recommended for teleconferences (e.g., Cyrs and Smith 1990; Monson 1978; Ostendorf 1989) as well as methods for increasing learner involvement in learning materials (e.g., advance organizers, self-assessment exercises). There are extensive guidelines available for interactive media (e.g., Lochte 1993; Schwier and Misanchuk 1993). Almost all such recommendations emphasize that interactivity must be planned or it is unlikely to occur (or be meaningful). The idea that interaction must be explicitly designed in distance education courses seems a difficult concept for many instructors to accept or understand.

Furthermore, any efforts to increase interactivity involve development and teaching efforts which must be taken into account. Even simple forms of interaction can take considerable time to prepare and carry out. When course enrollments are large, there are cost/benefit tradeoffs to be considered in providing interactivity (Dillon, Gibson, and Confessore 1991). Unless there are clear-cut benefits to adding interaction to a course, designers and instructors are not likely to invest the time to do so. In the absence of empirical evidence about the effects of interactivity on learning, such benefits are not well established.

Finally, we need to consider that the perception of interactivity may be as important as actual interaction. Fulford and Zhang (1993) examined learner perceptions in a course delivered by instructional television. They found that the critical predictor of student satisfaction in the course was not the extent of personal interaction but the perception of overall interaction. In other words, if students perceived that there had been a high level of student interaction in the course they were satisfied, regardless of how much interaction they had personally. This result suggests that the *potential* for interaction is an important design factor in distance education courses, even if most students do not take advantage of this potential.

A Case Study: The ETL/MEU Program

The Educational Technology Leadership (ETL) program is a Master's degree offered through Mind Extension University (MEU). All courses in the program are taught by faculty of the George Washington University in Washington, DC and delivered by instructional television to students across the country who receive the classes via cable, satellite, or videotaped format. In addition, all students are expected to use a computer bulletin board system (BBS) for completion of course assignments, exams, and discussions.

Interactivity occurs in two primary ways: telephone call-in during the television broadcasts (assuming that the student is watching the class live), and messages sent or received via the BBS. These are two very different forms of interaction. Telephone call-in allows students to provide and receive an immediate response to questions, whereas electronic messages involve delayed responses (one to two days). Call-ins are strictly auditory interaction while computer messages are written or typed. Telephone call-ins are always public and usually student-teacher interaction; electronic messages can be private and are often student-student or student-content interaction (i.e., databases or files). Finally, the occurrence of interaction via call-ins is restricted to weekly broadcast times but BBS interaction can occur anytime.

The cost/benefits of the two types of interaction are different as well. In order to provide the call-in capability, we have toll-free telephone lines and an audio technician to supervise the process. Each telephone call (five to ten minutes in duration) costs approximately $1 in toll charges, and we typically have fifteen to twenty calls per class; the labor costs of the audio technician are about $30 for a two hour class. So, we are spending about $50 per class to provide interaction via telephone call-in. Of course, this assumes the cost of purchasing a telephone bridge that allows multiple phone lines and real-time broadcasting of the classes via satellite so live interaction is possible. This latter consideration amounts to an expense of $800 per class for satellite time that could be saved if the classes were broadcast on a delayed basis (or distributed on videotape) with no interaction possible.

The costs of providing interaction via the BBS amount to the telephone charges associated with a toll-free line, plus the costs of a person to manage the BBS ("sysop") and the one-time cost of the BBS software and hardware. If each student spends an average of one hour per week using the BBS, the total telephone costs per semester are about $150 per student. Obviously, if students spend considerably more time on the BBS, or if class sizes are large, telephone costs can become appreciable. For this reason, we are encouraging students to obtain Internet accounts with unlimited monthly usage options (the BBS has an Internet gateway).

Responsibility for creating interactivity in the ETL program rests with the course instructors. In the case of the television broadcasts, faculty must build interactive sequences into their classes either in terms of simple question and answer sessions or more elaborate problem-solving or game activities. Similarly, in the case of the BBS, instructors must provide assignments and group activities that entail interaction. While the preparation time is not appreciable, the time required to conduct interactive segments and provide feedback can be significant. This is particularly a problem with the BBS because each message must be read and replied to. For example, if a class of thirty students completes an assignment and it takes the instructor twenty minutes to read and reply to each one, a total of ten hours is required to provide feedback to all students. If the class enrollment is large or there are many interactive activities, this can present a tremendous load on the instructor.

We do not have any data that tells us how the two kinds of interaction (call-ins during broadcasts and BBS messages) affect student achievement. We do know from evaluation studies that both kinds of interaction are valued by students and contribute to their satisfaction or dissatisfaction with the ETL program. Some of our students receive the television classes in videotape form and hence are not able to participate live. These students often report that they feel less involved in the class than other students. Most students who call-in during broadcasts or who are very active on the BBS say they find the opportunity to interact with the instructors and their classmates to be one of the best features of our program. On the other hand, students who do not receive timely feedback on their on-line assignments from the instructors become very frustrated. We feel that interactivity in the ETL program, when conducted properly by faculty, increases the motivation of students to complete courses.

Conclusions

It is difficult to make a cost/benefits evaluation of interactivity in the ETL program or in any distance education program. In the case of the ETL program, the direct costs of providing interaction are relatively modest: approximately $750 a course for the telephone call-ins during the television broadcasts and $150 per student for use of the BBS. The benefits are increased student involvement and satisfaction with the courses. However, there are many indirect costs associated with providing these interactive capabilities including the equipment needed and the expenses associated with satellite transmission or operating the BBS, as well as the instructor time required for preparation and completion. If only the direct costs are considered, the benefits would seem to easily outweigh the costs; however, if all of the items related to providing interactivity are taken into account, it may not be worthwhile. In the absence of evidence that interactivity has a significant effect on student achievement, it is not possible to make a better assessment. To make this determination, we need to conduct studies that measure the impact of different types of interactivity (e.g., telephone call-ins or BBS messages) on learning outcomes such as comprehension, retention, transfer, etc.

The cost/benefits of interactivity are likely to vary with different media, teaching strategies, types of learning, and groups of learners. For example, the costs of providing interaction via audioconferencing are relatively modest (i.e., telephone charges) but the possible benefits in terms of impact on learning are probably quite limited. On the other hand, creating interaction in a teleconference among individuals located at different sites could be quite expensive when the preparation time and satellite costs are taken into account. Some forms of interaction, such as simulations, games, or case studies, are more complicated to create but may also have greater impact on learning. Finally some groups of learners (e.g., young children, teenagers, senior executives, engineers, foreign students) may be more or less inclined to interact, and may derive varying degrees of benefit from such interaction. Therefore, the value of interaction needs to be assessed on a case by case basis for each distance education program.

References

Ahlm, M. 1972. Telephone instruction in distance education. *Epistolodidactica* 2:49–64.

Angell, D., and B. Heslop, 1994. *The Elements of E-mail Style.* Reading, MA: Addison-Wesley.

Barker, B. 1986. Interactive satellite instruction: How rural schools benefit. Little Rock, AR: Annual Conference of the Rural Education Association.

Beijer, E. 1972. A study of students' preferences with regard to different models of two-way communications. Epistolodidactica 2:83–90.

Cyrs, T. E., and F. A. Smith. 1990. *Teleclass Teaching: A Resource Guide.* 2d ed. Las Cruces, NM: New Mexico State University.

Dempsey, J. V., and G. C. Sales. 1994. *Interactive Instruction and Feedback.* Englewood Cliffs, NJ: Educational Technology Publications.

Dillon, C., C. Gibson, and S. Confessore. 1991. The economics of interaction in technology-based distance education. In *Proceedings of the Seventh Annual Conference on Distance Teaching and Learning.* Madison, WI: University of Wisconsin.

Flanders, N. A. 1970. *Analyzing Teacher Behavior.* Reading, MA: Addison-Wesley.

Fulford, C. P., and S. Zhang. 1993. Perceptions of interaction: The critical predictor in distance education. *The American Journal of Distance Education* 7(3):8–21.

Harasim, L. 1990. *Online Education: Perspectives on a New Environment.* New York: Praeger.

Lochte, R. H. 1993. *Interactive Television & Instruction.* Englewood Cliffs, NJ: Educational Technology Publications.

Massoumian, B. 1989. Successful teaching via two-way interactive video. *TechTrends* 34(2):16–19.

Monson, M. K. 1978. *Bridging the Distance.* Madison, WI: University of Wisconsin-Extension.

Moore, M. G. 1989. Three types of interaction. *The American Journal of Distance Education* 3(2):1–6.

Nichol, P. 1994. A descriptive study to determine the relationship between the nature of student interactivity and the scheme for learning in courses presented over live television. Washington, DC: The George Washington University.

Ostendorf, V. A. 1991. Increasing interactivity in live satellite events. *Teleconferencing News,* Sept/Oct.

Rekkedal, T. 1983. Written assignments in correspondence education: Effects of reducing turn-around time. An experimental study. *Distance Education* 4(2):231–252.

Rifkind, L. J. 1992. Immediacy as a predictor of teacher effectiveness in the instructional television classroom. *Journal of Interactive Television* 1(1):31–40.

Schwier, R. A., and E. Misanchuk. 1993. *Interactive Multimedia Instruction.* Englewood Cliffs, NJ: Educational Technology Publications.

Speth, C., J. Poggio, and D. Glassnapp. 1991. Midlands final evaluation report. Manhattan, KS: University of Kansas.

Stone, H. 1988. Variations in the characteristics and performance between on campus and video-based off-campus engineering graduate students. *Journal of Continuing Higher Education* 36(1):18–23.

Waggoner, M. 1992. *Empowering Networks: Computer Conferencing in Education.* Englewood Cliffs, NJ: Educational Technology Publications.

10 Linking Distance Education Theory to Learning Theory: A Systems Dynamic Approach to a Research Agenda on Learning Outcomes

Farhad Saba

The Universe refuses the deadening influence of complete conformity. And yet in its refusal, it passes towards novel order as a primary requisite for important experience.
—Alfred North Whitehead

Purpose

The future of distance education theory lies in its link to prevailing theories of learning, social theory, and communication theory[1]. Distance education theory is *complex,* and may better be described as a meta-theory comprised of the contributing theories required to explain it. Therefore, a *systems* (Bertalanffy 1968) approach is necessary to build a theory (Dubin 1978) of distance education, an approach which can do two things:

1. demonstrate the inter-relationship of various theoretical bodies comprising distance education, and
2. demonstrate such inter-relationships in a *dynamic* (time-based) form as the knowledge bases of comprising theoretical bodies grow and change over time.

This is a prodigious undertaking; one which can hardly be accomplished in the confines of the present paper. However, toward this end, a preliminary attempt will be made to link a contemporary theory of distance education with current theories of learning, and demonstrate their inter-relationships. In this,

I will use a systems *dynamic modeling* approach (Roberts et al. 1983) as my methodology.

Whitehead (1966) criticized the specialization of modern science by asserting, "As science grew, minds shrank in width of comprehension," and called for a "composite" notion of "understanding" (p. 44). The following paragraphs from Whitehead (1966) on the subject of understanding set the framework for the continuation of our discussion on *understanding* distance education through a dynamic systems method. He stated:

> In the first place, understanding always involves the notion of composition. This notion can enter in one of two ways. If the thing understood be composite, the understanding of it can be in reference to its factors, and to their ways of interweaving as so to form that total thing. This mode of comprehension makes evident why the thing is what it is.

> The second mode of understanding is to treat the thing as a unity, whether or not it is capable of analysis, and to obtain evidence as to its capacity for affecting its environment. The first mode may be called the internal understanding, and the second mode is the external understanding.

> But this phraseology tells only part of the tale. The two modes are reciprocal: either presupposes the other. The first mode conceives the thing as an outcome, the second mode conceives it as a causal factor. (pp. 45–46)

Dynamic, or time-based systems, are in perpetual process, and it is important to mention that Whitehead continued to state "It is true that nothing is finally understood until its reference to process has been made evident" (p. 46). Thus, in the analysis which will be presented here, concepts that are believed to comprise a system of distance education have at least two characteristics: 1) they are inter-related, and 2) they change over time. This also sets the framework for discussing learning *outcomes*. As Whitehead suggested above, outcome is an integral part of dynamic systems. Measuring learning outcomes, therefore, should be addressed in the overall context of our systems analysis. In other words, the interaction of the learner with his/her environment defines the outcome of learning at each point in time.

I will deal with these particular issues throughout this paper, and will set the stage for proposing a research agenda in the future, in which learning outcomes can be addressed in a dynamic and systemic way. It is sufficient to say at this point that currently, most measurements of learning outcomes are "snapshots" of the learner's ability at the moment that such abilities are measured. Furthermore, most measurements are not made within the context of the learner's life experience. These measurements, therefore, do not meet the criteria of "understanding" set by Whitehead, and are not sufficient for building and testing a contemporary theory of distance education.

Background

Although the practice of distance education may be as old as a hundred years, it is very young as an academic discipline. Keegan (1986) traced the academic origins of distance education to the mid 1970s. Among the few traditions which emerged at that time, he highlighted the pioneering research and practice of Charles A. Wedemeyer at the University of Wisconsin-Madison (p.7). Wedemeyer's studies were followed by Moore, who conducted a broad and comprehensive analysis of manuscripts related to adult education, distance education, correspondence education, and the use of telecommunications in education.

One result of this analysis was a study, published in 1973 (Moore 1973), in which Moore delineated a model of distance education. In this model, distance in education (or *transactional distance*) was defined not in terms of the geographical separation of the teacher and the learner, but as a function of the two variables, *structure and dialogue.* In other words, Moore demonstrated that the amount of distance in education was determined by how much the teaching-learning activity was open to learner independence (or dialogue), and how much it was confined to the responsiveness of an educational organization (or structure).

Saba (1989) applied a systems dynamic approach (Roberts et al. 1983) to Moore's concept of transactional distance, and suggested that a dynamic relationship existed between dialogue and structure. In other words, over a given period of time, as dialogue (learner control) increased, structure (instructor control) as well as transactional distance decreased; and as structure increased, dialogue decreased, but transactional distance increased. These hypotheses were tested by Saba and Shearer (1994) and were tentatively supported by the study.

Distance Education Theory and Learning Outcomes

Transactional distance, dialogue, and structure, however, are formal theoretical constructs which do not explain substantive outcomes of learning. For example, maximizing dialogue does not necessarily lead to increased mastery of a skill or knowledge domain. Or, maximizing structure may not provide the conditions necessary for exploratory learning. Therefore, at least two questions should be answered: 1) In any given period of time, what is the proper balance between dialogue and structure? and 2) how can learning theory inform distance education theory to determine such a proper balance?

Since such balance will determine the relationship of the learner as a sub-system with his/her environment, it will be instrumental in our understanding of learning outcomes of at least two kinds: goal-oriented or objective-based, and process oriented or exploratory learning. Once these questions have been answered, we can address the problem of learning outcomes and their measurement. It is in responding to these two questions, therefore, that we turn to in the remainder of this paper.

Methodology

In this section I will argue that the use of general systems theory is *essential,* as well as *central,* to the development of distance education as a *complex* theory. Dubin (1978) listed three criteria for complexity in a scientific model. A system is complex:

1. when there is a large number of units of analysis introduced into the model,
2. when there is exceptional form in one or more of the laws of interaction of the model, and
3. when there is a large number of system states that are specified for the model (pp. 253).

Dubin further explained that "Of course, any combination of these conditions would produce complexity in the model" (p. 253).

Distance education is a complex theory; its further growth and elaboration depends on its integration of other theoretical bodies such as learning, social, and communication theories. Integrating theories requires a methodology that is general enough to include various *attributes of units of theory,* and specific enough to provide for measuring variables of theoretical units (Dubin 1978).

In 1986 Bertalanffy summarized the "aims of general system theory" as follows:

- There is a general tendency towards integration in the various sciences, natural and social.
- Such integration seems to be centered in a general theory of systems.
- Such theory may be an important means for aiming at exact theory in the nonphysical fields of science.
- Developing unifying principles running "vertically" through the universe of individual sciences, this theory brings us nearer to the goal of unity of science.
- This can lead to a much-needed integration of scientific education (p. 38).

Thus, general systems theory is *essential* to building a theory of distance education because it provides for the integration of various theoretical attributes.

Systems theory is also *central* to a theory of distance education; it provides a means for including the inter-relationships of such attributes and variables. A core concept in distance education is the interaction between the teacher and the learner, between the learner and instructional materials, and among learners (Moore 1989). A thorough knowledge of the nature of these interactions is central to an understanding of distance education as a distinct area of scientific discipline. Dubin (1978) defines "a system to be any assemblage of elements that interact repeatedly and in the same manner when the identical elements are in contact with each other" (p. 240). Dubin continued to state that:

This definition has three components
1. A system is composed of defined elements that remain the same throughout the life of the system.
2. The elements describe the system because their systematic interactions with each other (laws of interaction) make it possible to characterize the states of the system.
3. In order for each of the elements of the system to be able to interact with at least one other element, the interactions take place within some defined boundary. (p. 240)

In distance education, it is the interactions of elements, i.e., dialogue, structure, and transactional distance, as delineated by Moore (1973, 1989), which make it possible to characterize it first, as a distinct area of scientific investigation, and second, as a system. In other words, dialogue, structure, and transactional distance are meaningful in relation to each other, and as separate parts cannot shed any light on how distance education may be described or how implementation parameters may be prescribed. As Saba and Shearer (1994) have tentatively demonstrated, transactional distance is a product of the inter-relationship of dialogue and structure. As an independent entity, it is hard, if not impossible, to conceptualize and measure transactional distance. Briggs and Peat (1989), in describing complex systems, stated "Complex systems both chaotic and orderly ones are ultimately unanalyzable, irreducible into parts, because the parts are constantly being folded into each other by iteration and feedback" (p. 147). Ironically, in understanding distance education, which is based on the "separation of the teacher and the learner" (Keegan 1986), it is important to move beyond the physical concept of distance, and turn the investigation to the understanding of transactional distance as a system concept.

Theories of Learning

The last fifty years have seen a tremendous growth in our knowledge of general psychology and the way we learn. This growth has been phenomenal in the last twenty-five years, as scientists have increasingly employed computers in researching cognition and artificial intelligence. The intent here is not to provide a summary of these theories of learning, but to address certain aspects of them that would eventually help us in linking learning theories to distance education theory.

Behaviorism. Traditionally, learning in education has been classified into the three domains of cognitive, affective (attitudinal), and psychomotor (Saettler 1990). This classification, initiated by the American Psychological Association in the mid 1940s, was to facilitate testing and measurement by standardizing the terminology associated with human behavior. The classification was designed to be closely related to behaviorism, which became the prevailing school of thought at the time: a theoretical view that primarily distinguished psychology from philosophy a century before, by objectifying the concept of learning, and continued to dominate the technology of education until the 1970s.

B. F. Skinner (1969) championed the objectification of learning by demonstrating the efficacy of reinforcement in shaping the learner's behavior. Although psychologists began to pay more attention to cognition in the 1950s, behaviorism gained steady popularity in educational practice. Defining learning as observable and demonstrable objectives was useful to educators in designing instructional systems that *directed* the learner toward attainment of specific *pre-determined* goals and the mastery of skills associated with those goals.

Cognition and Information Processing. Although behaviorism was successful in providing a modern structure for educational practice, as well as in influencing the advent of learning machines and the rise of programmed instruction and computer assisted instruction, it was woefully inadequate for explaining mental processes. Decision making, problem solving, and higher order thinking (e.g., meta-cognition and creativity) could not be adequately explained in behavioral terms.

Since the 1980s there has been tremendous growth in modeling the brain by computers, as well as in conceptualizing the brain as a computer. Such modeling efforts coupled with earlier mental models of the mind have resulted in two general explanations for how the brain works. These models, in general, either compare the brain to a small but massive parallel processing computer, or to a serial processor (Leahey and Harris 1993). In the former model, known as connectionism, the brain is described to be "a collection of simple but massively interconnected units [i.e., neurons]." In this model, "learning and cognition must be carried out by connectionist-type processes" (p. 307). This model, however, does not have an explanation for the logical and linguistic functions of the brain. Such functions are attributed to the latter model, or the symbolic system theory, which views the brain's function as serial processing of symbols and symbol systems.

In reconciling the two models Leahy and Harris (1993) stated:

> Yet we have learned, physically different computational systems may implement the same programs. Therefore it is possible that, although the brain is a massively parallel computer like a connection machine, the human mind in its rational aspects is a serial processor of representations, especially when thought is conscious. The more automatic and unconscious (intuitive) aspects of the human mind are connectionist in nature. Connectionist theories thus have a valuable role to play in being

the vital interface between symbol-system models of rational, rule-following thought, and intuitive, nonlinear, nonsymbolic thought. (p. 307)

Thus cognitive psychology shifted the focus from an empirical epistemology, which viewed knowledge acquisition in a simple stimulus–response–reinforcement model, to a more subjective model, in which the learner participated in knowledge formation by relating new information to prior knowledge, and by employing other processes such as reasoning, decision making, and problem solving.

Constructivism: Attitude, Intentionality and Teleological Behavior. Cognitive science, at least in its present stage of development, does not directly address the question of purposeful behavior and free will. It leaves the following question unanswered to a large degree: If all human behavior is *dependent* on prior knowledge and environmental stimuli, how can we explain independent action and autonomous human behavior? An adequate response to this question is important for a coherent theory of distance education, since learner autonomy is a cornerstone of adult learning theory, a concept that is increasingly extended to K-12, and other educational arenas.

American pragmatist philosophers and psychologists of the late nineteenth and early twentieth century have addressed the issue of independent human behavior and its ramifications for teaching and learning (Murphy 1990). Among them the work of John Dewey and William James are outstanding. However, as Saettler (1990) has pointed out, a full analysis of Dewey's psychology of learning has not been accomplished yet. Furthermore, current general educational psychology textbooks make only a cursory reference to Dewey and mention James even less.

It seems that the emerging paradigm of constructivism (Jonassen 1991; Lebow 1993) is either based on pragmatism or is greatly influenced by it. In other words, if constructivism is not a full implementation of pragmatism it is the closest model of learning that has emerged from it so far. This model of learning views the learner as an independent agent who in his or her *experience* of objects and events encounters questions, formulates hypotheses, and seeks to resolve such questions by testing the hypotheses. Resolution of the problem both requires *action* and may result in action on the part of the learner, which effects his/her immediate environment, leading to new questions and new hypotheses. This experience is subjective, and therefore highly individual. The learner may seek additional information while looking for a solution or testing a hypothesis, but the *content of instructional material* is meaningful in the *context* of the problem. This learning process unfolds itself during one's life experience. Therefore such learning, by definition, is life-long, self-directed, situated in the context of one's life experience, and highly independent.

Recently, several models of teaching and learning, which had proven to be effective in the past, have re-emerged as constructivism has gained popularity among instructional designers and educators. For example, situated learning, a concept familiar to adult educators, has now been extended to K-12 education. Also, cognitive apprenticeship, a concept based on the age-old practice in trades and crafts, has been adapted to several educational settings. In such scenarios students are presented with a problem similar to what they may find in an "authentic" situation; they receive guidance and feedback from the instructor in their search for a solution to the problem (Alvarez et al. 1990; Brown et al. 1988; Collins 1988; Farmer et al. 1992; Stinson 1990; Young and Kulikowich 1992).

Implications of Learning Theories for the Dynamic Theory of Distance Education

Behaviorism, cognitivism, and constructivism suggest a continuum that ranges from objective-based teaching to exploratory learning. On the objective end of the continuum, the learner is a novice in need of direct instruction, to begin forming schema for new knowledge domains, and to connect new concepts to the ones s/he has already acquired. In this case, it is hypothesized that *structure* is high, and *dialogue* is low. The learner requires *direct* instruction, and shows low *activity* to keep the *dialogue* low and *structure* high. As the learner develops new schemata and can relate them to prior knowledge, s/he gains the confidence to engage in *independent* exploration of the new knowledge domain, forms her/his own mini-hypotheses, tests them and observes the *outcomes*. Over a period of time as the teaching-learning process unfolds—for example, in a telelesson or a course of study comprised of several telelessons—*it is hypothesized, that dialogue will increase and structure decrease as the novice learner approaches mastery and expertise*. The instructor, therefore, becomes more of a manager of instruction than the purveyor of information. Eventually, as the learner attains more expertise, the learner and the instructor become collaborators and the instructional system gains *equilibrium*. At this point the teaching-learning process may terminate, or may continue as a collegial relationship. These hypotheses, however, only explain the relationship of the instructor and the learner, but do not shed much light on learner-learner interaction, or learner-subject interaction. We turn our attention to these two matters now.

In what seems to be an extension of biological–psychological theory of connectionism to a social theory of connectionism, Vygotski proposed the concept of the zone of proximal development. Woolfolk (1993), in describing Vygotski's idea, said

> The **zone of proximal development** is the area where the child cannot solve a problem alone but can be successful under adult guidance or in collaboration with a more advanced peer.... For Vygotski, social interaction was more than a method of teaching– it was the origin of higher mental processes such as problem solving. He assumed that 'the notion of mental function can properly be applied to group as well as individual forms of activity'

(Wetsch, 1991, p. 27) For example, Vygotski believed groups could 'remember'. (p. 48–49)

The concept of the zone of proximal development provides the theoretical basis for extending the dynamic theory of distance education to include peer interaction. The 1994 study by Saba and Shearer involved only one-on-one interaction. The dynamic model should now be expanded to include peer interaction.

The subject of learner-content interaction should also be addressed, as computer and telecommunication technologies promise to provide the technological infrastructure to greatly enhance the interaction of learners with massive international data bases. So far, in traditional education as well as in most distance education programs, learner-content interaction has been limited to print materials, or linear film and video. Rarely have distance education organizations employed interactive multimedia to an extent which would have a serious impact on the field. Most distance education, despite all of the new technological developments, is one-way video, two-way audio.

The global Internet, however, is bound to change this situation. For the first time, the network, and new interface software such as Mosaic™ and Netscape™, has provided the means for the learner and the instructor to access information on demand, as the teaching-learning situation may require. In other words, both the learner and the instructor are potentially capable of accessing information that is meaningful to them in the context in which they are communicating and at a level appropriate to the developmental stage of the learner. Furthermore, new software, such as AppleScript™ in the case of the Macintosh computer, provides a means for linking the interface software to customized data bases which would track the learner's progress, provide a sand box for the learner to explore, and eventually create a simulated environment for contextualized and situated learning[2].

At this point, we are a few years away from attaining the goal of being able to differentially personalize information on a specific topic for learners. Despite the growth of the Internet, organized digital information is still scarce. Although we can find a great amount of information on the network, being able to build a "curriculum" based on the available information is another matter. Nevertheless, the potential is there as publishers shed their fear of digital "publishing" and make their books available on the net, and as authors decide to publish their new materials in digital format (Negroponte 1995). When more organized information becomes available on the net, both the instructor and the learner will be able to search and find relevant information as the learning situation at each particular point in time may demand. **This situated, time-based crafting of the moment of teaching and learning *experience* as the instructional/learning process unfolds is the primary idea behind the dynamic theory of distance education.**

Verifying the Link Between Distance Education Theory and Theories of Learning

I posed two questions earlier in this paper and now will address them directly. These were: 1) In any given period of time, what is the proper balance between dialogue and structure? and 2) how can learning theory inform distance education theory to determine such a proper balance?

In light of our discussion, the relevance of learning theory to distance education theory lies in

- the process of the definition of goals in teaching and learning,
- who defines the goals,
- how they are articulated, and
- whether they are attributed to dialogue or structure.

In other words, in understanding distance education systems, we should examine, for each session of instruction,

- to what extent the goals are pre-determined for the learner,
- what "objectives" the learner is expected to achieve, and
- to what extent the learner is allowed (or the learner chooses) to exercise his/her freedom to explore beyond the set goals or explore new possibilities within the set goals.

It is important to note here that our analysis is purely descriptive. At this point in this project, there should be no attempt to make prescriptive principles for the design of new distance education systems based on the ideas presented so far. Prescriptive principles can only be suggested when the propositions here are formalized, hypotheses are derived from them, and the hypotheses are put to test by data collection, data analysis, and synthesis of the results.

Such data collection and analysis is at the core of the issue of measuring learning outcomes when such outcomes are exploratory, and their manifestation in the action of the learner may not occur in the immediate future. In resolving this issue, I turn to Whitehead (1966) again. He stated, "The data of our experience are of two kinds. They can be analyzed into realized matter-of-fact and into potentialities for matter-of-fact" (p. 94). It is capturing such potentialities in data that should be addressed if this project is to continue.

A combination of the developments in technology and the promise of constructivist instructional design may lead us to create instruments for data collection for open ended learning. For instance, as it was suggested before, a combination of the Internet World Wide Web browsers, programs which enable us to make use of several types of software in combination (e.g., AppleScript™), and data base software such as Filemaker Pro™, can be used to develop a learning space in which the learners' "procedural actions" in reasoning, decision making, and note taking for monitoring self-learning (meta-cognition) and its development can be captured and analyzed (B. Dodge personal communication, March 13, 1995). Such data can then be simulated using STELLA™ (a system dynamics modeling and simulation software) which would project the *potential* of the data into the future, based on the available data captured at a specific point in the history of the "subject." This extrapolation, however, will remain probabilistic, until it is transformed to matter-of-fact by the learner's action in a future point in time. For such an experiment to be successful, it must be conducted in a naturalistic context, where the learner makes use of the Internet regularly, and when a reasonable amount of information for exploration by the learner can be accessed. My research associate, Rick Shearer, and I hope to develop an experiment based on the ideas in this presentation and attempt to verify the link between learning theories and the dynamic theory of distance education in the near future.

References

Alvarez, M. C., and others. 1990. Case-based instruction and learning: An interdisciplinary project. Paper presented at the Annual Meeting of the College Reading Association, Nashville, TN. ERIC Document Reproduction Service, ED 326 837.

Bertalanffy, L. V. 1968. *General System Theory: Foundations, Development, Application.* New York: George Braziller.

Briggs, J., and F. D. Peat. 1989. *Turbulent Mirror: An Illustrated Guide to Chaos Theory and the Science of Wholeness.* New York: Harper & Row.

Brown, J. S., and others. 1988. Situated cognition and the culture of learning No. 120; 141). BBN Labs, Inc., Cambridge, MA, and Xerox Corporation, Palo Alto, CA, Palo Alto Research Center. ERIC Document Reproduction Service, ED 342 357.

Collins, A. 1988. Cognitive apprenticeship and instructional technology. No. 120; 143). BBN Labs, Inc., Cambridge, MA.

Dubin, R. 1978. *Theory Building* (rev. ed.). New York: The Free Press.

Farmer, J. A., Jr., and others. 1992. *Cognitive Apprenticeship: Implications for Continuing Professional Education. New Directions for Adult and Continuing Education,* 55 (Fall), 41–49.

Jonassen, D. H. 1991. Objectivism versus constructivism: Do we need a new philosophical paradigm? *Educational Technology Research and Development* 39(3):5–14.

Keegan, D. 1986. *Foundations of Distance Education.* London: Routledge.

Leahey, T. H., and R. J. Harris. 1993. *Learning and Cognition*. 3d ed. Englewood Cliffs, NJ: Prentice Hall.

Lebow, D. 1993. Constructivist values for instructional systems design: Five principles towards a new mindset. *Educational Technology Research and Development* 41(3): 4–16.

Moore, M. G. 1973. Towards a theory of independent learning and teaching. *Journal of Higher Education* 44(9):661–79.

Moore, M. G. 1989. Three types of learning. In *Readings in Principles of Distance Education*, eds. M. G. Moore and G. C. Clark, 100–105. University Park, PA: The American Center for the Study of Distance Education.

Murphy, J. 1990. *Pragmatism: From Peirce to Davidson*. Boulder, CO: Westview Press.

Negroponte, N. 1995. *Being Digital*. New York: Alfred A. Knopf.

Roberts, N., D. F. Andersen, R. M. Deal, M. S. Garet, and W. A. Shaffer. 1983. *Introduction to Computer Simulation: The Systems Dynamic Approach*. Reading, MA: Addison-Wesley.

Saba, F. 1989. Integrated telecommunications and instructional transaction. *The American Journal of Distance Education* 2(3):17–24.

Saba, F., and R. Shearer. 1994. Verifying key theoretical concepts in a dynamic model of distance education. *The American Journal of Distance Education* 8(1):36–59.

Saettler, P. 1990. *The Evolution of American Educational Technology*. Englewood, CO: Libraries Unlimited.

Skinner, B. F. 1969. *Contingencies of Reinforcement*. New York: Appleton-Century-Crofts.

Stinson, J. E. 1990. Integrated contextual learning: Situated learning in the business profession. Paper presented at the Annual Meeting of the American Educational Research Association, Boston, MA. ERIC Document Reproduction Service, ED 319 330.

Wagner, E. D. 1994. In support of a functional definition of interaction. *The American Journal of Distance Education* 8(2):6–29.

Whitehead, A. N. 1966. *Modes of Thought*. New York: Free Press.

Woolfolk, A. E. 1993. *Educational Psychology*. 5th ed. Boston: Allyn and Bacon.

Young, M. F., and J. M. Kulikowich. 1992. Anchored instruction and anchored assessment: An ecological approach to measuring situated learning. Paper presented at the Annual Meeting of the American Educational Research Association, San Francisco, CA. ERIC Document Reproduction Service, ED 354 269.

Notes:

1. For example, Wagner (1994) discussed the relevance of communication theory to the concept of interactivity in distance education.
2. I must acknowledge informal conversations with two colleagues: Bernard Dodge, who conceptualized the combination of browser software, AppleScript, and data base software for management of on-line constructivist instruction, and is in the process of implementing his idea; and Brockenbrough Allen, for his insightful comments on constructivist learning, case-based learning and situated instruction.

The Human Element in Distance Education: Instructional Interaction, Self-Directed Learning, and Empowerment Revisited

Frank Tallman

But there are other important points to note in talking about the academy. We know it's not only a place where there's tremendous competition for status and prestige, but that humanistic intellectuals are actually losing this competition. We know we're being marginalized vis-à-vis the technological intelligentsia. More and more we feel that what we have to offer has very little to do with the crucial role that science and technology play in advanced capitalist society. Cornel West (p. 92)

Introduction

I believe Cornel West has articulated the major challenge facing distance educators in the current environment. With the advent of sophisticated communications and information management technology, it becomes increasingly easy to provide instructional services to a greater number of students. It is critical that the value of the human element within the instructional transaction not be lost or denigrated by the din of technological proliferation or the need for industrial efficiency. Distance instruction offered through institutions of higher education has a responsibility to sustain the critical priority of human beings in a democratic society. The responsibility includes the domestication of technological innovation for the betterment of humanity.

Contributions from Research in Distance Teaching and Learning

The literature is not wanting of suggestions for improving the instructional process in distance education. Sammons (1991), Wagner (1990), and Davis (1990) recommend that instructional designers and instructors use the many resources of cognitive psychology. These resources include instructional design methodologies, media selection, instructional theory, psychological research on text comprehension, the use of schemata, and concept maps. Duning, Van Kekerix, and Zaborowski (1993) and Chute, Balthazar, and Poston (1990) consider the implications of telecommunications and the possibilities this brings to the instructional process in distance education. Verduin and Clark (1991) address the spectrum of instructional considerations in terms of a "perceptual approach" in their discussion of distance teaching. This includes a brief examination of behavior (cognitive, affective, and psychomotor), instructional delivery systems, and the communication system. Garrison and Shale's edited work (1990) includes chapters addressing such diverse aspects of distance instruction as course creation, audio teleconferencing, communications technology, video-based instruction, and media and instructional methods. Others such as Fulford and Zhang (1993), St. Pierre (1989), Chacon-Duque (1985), and Tallman (1994) pursue the relationship between instructional effectiveness and student satisfaction. Munro (1991) considers presence at a distance, Moore (1983) offers the idea of transactional distance, and Holmberg (1989) acknowledges the importance of "guided didactic conversation"—all deal with the relationship between the learner and the instructor in terms of interaction.

Evident in all the aforementioned discussions is the intent to provide the learner with the possibility for an optimal distance learning experience. All agree that the substance of learning is integrally related to the delivery or method of learning. It might also be argued that in no case is the distance instructional event an isolated event. It is always an occurrence related to the larger social world, it is only one moment in the learner's quest for knowledge.

Because learning is a social phenomenon, its implications supersede existential benefits for the learner and the mere one-way transmission of knowledge by the instructor. There is a responsibility, an ethical imperative, to instruct and learn in a praxis-defined contingency. Miller (1990) rightly notes that lifelong learning is integral to sustaining democracy. He goes on to aver

> If we in distance education take seriously our social role, we must also take seriously the task of integrating our delivery mechanisms with the content and processes of learning and the special needs and strengths of our students. (p. 219)

The instructional interaction is at the heart of the educational process. Garrison and Shale (1990) support the place of academic discourse and dialogue in distance instruction. The research base for providing authentic socially-grounded instruction in which the learner is empowered to be both independent and interdependent is present. It is possible, quite simply, to address all three types of academic conversation proposed by Ehrmann (1988). These are

- the creative, interactive use of the tools, resources, and didactic materials of the field;

- timely (instantaneous) conversation about what is being learned with the faculty and other students; and

- time-delayed conversation about what is being learned, through the exchange of homework and projects, and the receipt of feedback. (p. 1)

Closely related to the contributions from distance education research are contributions from the field of adult learning.

Contributions from Adult Learning

Certainly the contributions which may be gleaned from the expansive field of adult education and applied to the development and delivery of effective instruction via distance education are many. Arguably, the major contribution is the idea of self-directed learning and the research defining the self-directed learner. The literature contains several different definitions and perspectives of self-directed learning (Brockett and Hiemstra 1991; Knowles 1975; Mezirow 1983; Moore 1980). Inherent in all these definitions is the concept that self-directedness reflects psychological development (Tennant 1991). Candy (1991) asserts an expanded definition in which the learner is an active participant in the construction of knowledge through mutually interdependent interaction with that learner's environment. The learner displays personal autonomy, self-management, active participation in conducting the learning experience, and learning in the natural setting. In this model knowledge is temporal and socially constructed. This view brings a redefined notion of instruction; one which is socially aware, action-oriented, and reflexive.

Caffarella (1993) proposes three ways self-directed learning has contributed to our understanding of learning. These are "(1) identifying an important form of adult learning and providing us with insights into the process of learning, (2) challenging us to define and debate the salient characteristics of adult learners, and (3) expanding our thinking about learning in formal settings" (p. 27). The incorporation of what we know about adult learning into the instructional process is an absolute necessity. It is not possible to provide effective instruction without understanding the process of learning and the characteristics of our students. But the specific task at hand is to incorporate what we know into the formal instructional setting.

Knowles (1975) and others (Brockett and Hiemstra 1991; Brookfield 1991; Candy 1991; Garrison 1992; Hiemstra and Sisco 1990) argue for the priority of the learner in the learning transaction. Brookfield's (1991) development of "grounded teaching" relies upon the characteristics of the self-directed learner. He acknowledges that the "most important characteristic of grounded teaching is that it is based on an understanding of, concern for, and attention to the learner's experience of learning" (p. 35). The teacher and learner are in a reflexive relationship in which the teacher's actions are in response to the learner who in turn responds to the instructional frame. If this is indeed a valid proposal then strict instructional designs which do not allow for learner priority and do not facilitate an instructor-learner dialectic are impervious to the call for effective instruction. In this dialectical relationship the teacher is able to exhibit credibility by using content mastery and pedagogical understanding as means for helping the learner become self-directed and for providing an environment for learning.

Candy (1991) hinges the idea of self-directed learning to constructivist theory. This sharing of assumptions means that the learner choice to engage in a particular learning activity indicates an intentional and logical act by the learner. Candy also notes that for the instructor to "enter into the perspective of the learner" requires understanding instructional events from the learner's point of view. The instructor is posed with the problem of understanding the learner's point of view in order to help the learner to understand inappropriate structures, faulty logic, or dysfunctional beliefs so that the learner has both the possibility and the opportunity to change. The instructor, by recognizing these assumptions, recognizes and respects the learner as a person who is contributing to the learning transaction.

The decision by the instructor to engage in this type of constructivist learning is an educational intervention accompanied by an ethical mandate. The idea of value-free knowledge or pedagogy is necessarily discarded. According to Candy, self-directed learning enables the learner to identify learning purposes, to use learning resources, and to manage one's learning. The instructor provides a psychosocial environment in which the learner can assume increasingly greater control of learning. In this structure it is apparent that both the learner and the learning are particular and specific. One must ask whether it is possible that pre-packaged curricula might, in fact, prevent the learner from transcending the safety of the information given and limit the learner to mere reproduction of knowledge rather than provoke knowledge production.

There are many tools that can be integrated into the instructional sequence and will encourage self-directed learning. Galbraith and Zelenak (1991, 103) note discussion as "perhaps the most widely preferred method." They also identify the case method, learning contracts, critical incident learning, and mentoring as available and appropriate techniques. Other techniques identified in recent literature include journalizing, cognitive apprenticeships, independent learning projects, bibliographic instruction, and the use of various types of instructional technology (Blackwood and White 1991; Brandt, Farmer, and Buckmaster 1993; Candy 1991; Merriam and Caffarella 1991; Stouch 1993). A tool which is not often addressed in the literature of self-directed learning but one which holds great promise for developing self-directed learners is the "Knowledge Vee" developed by Novak and Gowin (1984). All these tools are suitable for facilitating self-directed learning.

Brockett (1991) extends the idea of self-directed learning to professional development for the instructor. He contends that professional development is both a responsibility to keep current (in both content and pedagogically related fields) and a critically reflective experience. Brockett offers several means by which the instructor can engage these events. These include: professional reading, professional writing, professional associations, and electronic networks. These intentional and often dialogical efforts enable the instructor to be self-directed and to evade the possibility of assuming a reactive role in the educational process.

The research and literature addressing self-directed learning holds much promise for instructional development and improvement in distance education. Instructors who recognize and respect their students, who facilitate proactive learning, and who take seriously the ethical mandate inherent in the instructional transaction provide an environment in which Lindeman's (1926) assertion is realized.

> Life is experiencing and intelligent living is a way of making experience an educational adventure. To be educated is not to be informed but to find illumination in informed living. Periods of intellectual awakening are correctly named "enlightenments" for it is then that lovers of wisdom focus the light of learning upon experience and thereby discover new meanings for life, new reasons for living. (p. 110)

Contributions from Critical Theory

Contemporary critical theory is deeply founded in the idea that human life must be transformed. Welton (1993) traces this belief back to the Institute of Social Research in Frankfurt and its adherents, Adorno, Marcuse, Horkheimer, and Benjamin. In this respect human knowledge is emancipatory and dynamic. Fundamental to this paradigm is the Habermasian notion that instruction is not merely the passing on of a body of information but rather "the outcome of human activity motivated by interests that guide and shape their learning processes" (Welton 1993, 83).

Making of meaning is assumptively pragmatic and the symbolic interactive character of the learning transaction between learner and teacher displays the inherently problematic nature of knowledge. This is no less true of learning and instruction carried on in a distance environment than learning and instruction conducted in a face-to-face encounter. It is, however, of paramount importance that the distance instructor define instruction so as to acknowledge the problematic character of knowledge. This definition includes Giroux's (1981) assertion that

> knowledge should be viewed as a shared process, a mediation between teachers and students, a creative political exchange that forges commonalities and the kind of critical reflection that allows all to be seen as both teachers and learners. (p. 68)

The ground of dialogue becomes an ethical mandate for action rather than a simplified set of context-free ideas that are merely transmitted to a non-reflective learner. The appropriate separation of learner and instructor must not include a separation of knowledge and context.

The possibility for distance instruction brings with it both an avenue for empowering learners and facilitating learning and a threat to the necessary ethical imperative of the human learning transaction. Bellah and his colleagues (1991) ably present this dilemma.

> Technological development and affluence, which are related to our deepest problems, can also, if used rightly, enlarge the possibilities for our fulfillment in work and as citizens, for democratic participation and committed family lives, even for the space to develop genuine spirituality. (p. 50)

For distance instructors this very real dilemma is one which deserves serious consideration. This is a point that requires the distance education instructor to reflectively consider her or his own assumptions regarding the instructional process. Maxine Greene (1973) states

> Teaching is purposeful action . . . intentions will inevitably be affected by the assumptions he makes regarding human nature and human possibility. Many of these assumptions are hidden; most have never been activated. If he is to achieve clarity and full consciousness, the teacher must attempt to make such assumptions explicit; for only then can they be examined analyzed and understood. (p. 69–70)

It is this reflection that allows the instructor to present human solutions to human problems. Benne (1990) articulately illustrates the danger of providing a technological solution to a human problem. He contends that if this alien solution is allowed technology will become the new faith, a faith that will prevail if only the final obstacle can be overcome. That obstacle is the human being.

Of course, neither Habermas nor Benne are arguing for the abandonment of technology in the instructional process. However, they are advocating a human(e) instructional process that is not dominated by the tyranny of technology but is empowered by a moral educational community. With West (1993) we contend for the rightful place for technology. A humane environment recognizing the primacy of the individual supported by sophisticated technology. Giroux (1993) contends for a similar moral and human center to the instructional process. He declares

> . . . reform proposals that pit a romanticized view of the laws and logic of the market against the discourse of ethics, political agency, and social responsibility. . . .calls for schools to be dispensers of an unproblematic cultural tradition in which the emergence of cultural differences is seen as a sign of fragmentation and a departure from rather than an advance towards democracy. (p. 12)

Instruction is democratic to the extent that it encourages learners to understand and know in order to construct and share power over those institutions that govern their lives. Therefore, through education at a distance, instructors have the opportunity to expand the boundaries of democracy by engaging themselves and their students in discourse which actively advocates equality, justice, and freedom. It is this concept of the instructor as cultural worker and instruction as cultural work which enables human potential and substantiates democratic process. The importance of authentic dialogue in the instructional process cannot be overstated. I believe this is particularly vital to the instructional event carried via distance education as is pointed out by Hall (1991) when he writes "only when there is an Other can you know who you are . . . and there is no identity . . . without the dialogic process" (p. 15).

Critical theory encourages distance instruction that is firmly and deeply rooted in the reflective activity of the instructor and purposefully and intentionally seeks to empower distance learners rather than domesticate them. Critical theory recognizes the inherently political and ethical attributes of the instructional process and with Whitehead (1954) advocates university [distance] instruction that

> imparts information, but imparts it imaginatively. At least, this is the function it should perform for society. This atmosphere of excitement, arising from imaginative consideration, transforms knowledge. A fact is no longer a bare fact: it is invested with all its possibilities. It is no longer a burden on the memory: it is energizing as the poet of our dreams, and as the architect of our purposes. (p. 93)

Implications for Research in Distance Education Instruction

If one affirms the priority of humanity in the instructional process and the contingent relationship between the individual and society then future research must take as its methodological assumptions forms which acknowledge this priority. The various modes of qualitative inquiry hold great promise for the development of distance instruction.

As well, based in the rapid growth in the number of learners studying via distance education and the relatively limited number of instructors available, future research should investigate the integration of technological forms which will facilitate instruction without hindering human interaction.

The research literature would be well served by portraying the stories of distance education students and instructors in their pursuit of lifelong learning. The narratives might present key aspects of instructional transactions, the value of mentoring, chronicle the development of reflective practice by both learner and instructor, or some other aspect of the instructional process.

Finally, the possibility of instruction as a means of encouraging social responsibility and sustaining democratic practice as explicated in contemporary critical theory surely holds great promise.

A Concluding Comment

Distance education instruction includes a portentous mandate. In an age characterized by distance, the possibility of transcending spatial limitations with legitimate human interaction is exciting and inspiring. Technological innovation appears poised to enhance the human element necessary to legitimate distance instructional interactions. Smith and Small (1982) capture the essence of the possibility and the responsibility that faces distance instructors.

> In our view it is unfortunate that some systems are expending vast amounts of time and money trying to devise learning packages which will allow students to become completely independent of teachers and other students. In these systems the notion of learning as a social experience has not received the consideration we believe it warrants. (p. 139)

References

Bellah, R., R. Madsen, W. Sullivan, A. Swidler, and S. Tipton. 1992. *The Good Society*. New York: Vintage Books.

Benne, K. 1990. *The Task of Post-contemporary Education.* New York: Teacher's College Press.

Blackwood, C., and B. White. 1991. Technology for teaching and learning improvement. In *Facilitating Adult Learning: A Transactional Process,* ed. M. W. Galbraith, 135–162. Malabar, FL: Kreiger Publishing.

Brandt, B., J. Farmer, and A. Buckmaster. 1993. Cognitive apprenticeship approach to helping adults learn. In *Applying Cognitive Learning Theory to Adult Learning. New Directions for Adult and Continuing Education,* 59, ed. D. D. Flannery, 69–78. San Francisco: Jossey-Bass.

Brockett, R., 1991. Strategies and resources for improving the instructional process. In *Facilitating Adult Learning: A Transactional Process,* ed. M. W. Galbraith, 193–212. Malabar, FL: Kreiger Publishing.

Brockett, R., and R. Hiemstra. 1991. *Self-direction in Adult Learning: Perspectives on Theory, Research, and Practice.* New York: Routledge.

Brookfield, S. 1991. Grounding teaching in learning. In *Facilitating Adult Learning: A Transactional Process,* ed. M. W. Galbraith, 33–56. Malabar, FL: Kreiger Publishing.

Caffarella, R. 1993. Self-directed learning. In *New Directions in Adult and Continuing Education: An update on Adult Learning Theory,* 57, ed. S. B. Merriam, 25–36. San Francisco: Jossey-Bass.

Candy, P. 1991. *Self-direction for Lifelong Learning.* San Francisco: Jossey-Bass.

Chacon-Duque, F. 1985. A multivariate model for evaluating distance higher education. Unpublished doctoral dissertation, The Pennsylvania State University, University Park, PA.

Chute, A., L. Balthazar, and C. Poston. 1990. Learning from teletraining: What AT&T research says. In *Contemporary Issues in American Distance Education,* ed. M. G. Moore, 260–276. New York: Pergamon Press.

Davis, D. 1990. Text comprehension: Implications for the design of self-instructional materials. In *Contemporary Issues in American Distance Education,* ed. M. G. Moore, 243–259. New York: Pergamon Press.

Duning, B., M. Van Kekerix, and L. Zaborowski. 1993. *Reaching Learners Through Telecommunications.* San Francisco: Jossey-Bass.

Ehrmann, S. 1988. Technologies for access and quality: An agenda for three conversations. Washington, DC: Annenberg/CPB Project.

Fulford, C., and S. Zhang. 1993. Perceptions of interaction: The critical predictor in distance education. *The American Journal of Distance Education* 7(3):8–21.

Galbraith, M., and B. Zelenak. 1991. Adult learning methods and techniques. In *Facilitating Adult Learning: A Tansactional Process,* ed. M. W. Galbraith, 33–56. Malabar, FL: Kreiger Publishing.

Garrison, D. R. 1992. Critical thinking and self-directed learning in adult education: An analysis of responsibility and control issues. *Adult Education Quarterly* 42:136–148.

Garrison, D. R., and D. Shale. 1990. *Education at a Distance: From Issues to Practice.* Malabar, FL: Krieger.

Giroux, H. 1981. *Ideology, Culture, and the Process of Schooling.* Philadelphia: Temple University Press.

Giroux, H. 1993. *Living Dangerously: Multiculturalism and the Politics of Difference.* New York: Peter Lang Publishing.

Greene, M. 1973. *The Teacher as Stranger: Educational Philosophy for the Modern Age.* Belmont, CA: Wadsworth.

Hall, S. 1991. Ethnicity: Identity and difference. *Radical America.* 13(4):9–20.

Hiemstra, R., and B. Sisco. 1990. *Individualizing Instruction: Making Learning Personal, Empowering, and Successful.* San Francisco: Jossey-Bass.

Holmberg, B. 1989. The concept, basic character and development potentials of distance education. *Distance Education* 10(1):127–134.

Knowles, M. 1975. *Self-directed Learning: A Guide for Learners and Teachers.* New York: Association Press.

Lindeman, E. C. 1926. *The Meaning of Adult Education.* New York: New Republic, Inc.

Merriam, S. B., and R. S. Caffarella. 1991. *Learning in Adulthood: A Comprehensive Guide.* San Francisco: Jossey-Bass.

Mezirow, J. 1983. A critical theory of adult learning and education. In *Adult Learning and Education,* ed. M. Tight. London: Croom Helm.

Miller, G. 1990. Distance education and the curriculum: Dredging a new mainstream. In *Contemporary Issues in American Distance Education,* ed. M. G. Moore, 211–220. New York: Pergamon Press.

Moore, M. G. 1980. Independent study. In *Redefining the Discipline of Adult Education,* eds. R. D. Boyd, J. W. Apps, and Associates. San Francisco: Jossey-Bass.

Moore, M. G. 1983. On a theory of independent study. In *Distance Education: International Perspectives,* eds. D. Sewart, D. Keegan, and B. Holmberg, 68–94. London: Croom Helm.

Munro, J. 1991. Presence at a distance: The educator-learner relationship in distance education and dropout. Unpublished doctoral dissertation. The University of British Columbia, Canada.

Novak, J., and D. Gowin. 1984. *Learning How to Learn.* New York: Cambridge University Press.

Sammons, M. 1991. Strategies for improving instructional design. In *The Foundations of American Distance Education: A Century of Correspondence Study,* eds. B. Watkins and S. Wright. Dubuque, IA: Kendall/Hunt.

Smith, K., and I. Small. 1982. Student support: How much is enough. In *Learning at a Distance: A World Perspective,* eds. J. S. Daniel, M. A. Stroud and J. R. Thompson. Edmonton: Athabasca University.

St. Pierre, S. 1989. Student perception of the effectiveness of correspondence instruction. Unpublished doctoral dissertation, The Pennsylvania State University, University Park, PA.

Stouch, C. 1993. What instructors need to know about learning how to learn. In *New Directions for Adult and Continuing Education: Applying Cognitive Learning Theory to Adult Learning,* 59, ed. D. Flannery, 59–69. San Francisco: Jossey-Bass.

Tallman, F. 1994. Satisfaction and completion in correspondence study: The influence of instructional and student support services. *The American Journal of Distance Education* 8(2):43–57.

Tennant, M. 1991. The psychology of adult teaching and learning. In *Adult Education: Evolution and Achievements in a Developing Field of Study,* eds. J. M. Peters, P. Jarvis, and Associates, 191–216. San Francisco: Jossey-Bass.

Verduin, J., and T. Clark. 1991. *Distance Education: The Foundations of Effective Practice.* San Francisco: Jossey-Bass.

Wagner, E. 1990. Instructional design and development: Contingency management for distance education. In *Contemporary Issues in American Distance Education,* ed. M. G. Moore, 298–312. New York: Pergamon Press.

Welton, M. 1993. The contribution of critical theory to our understanding of adult learning. In *New directions in Adult and Continuing Education: An Update on Adult Learning Theory,* 57, ed. S. B. Merriam, 81–90. San Francisco: Jossey-Bass.

West, C. 1993. *Prophetic Thought in Postmodern Times.* Monroe, ME: Common Courage Press.

Whitehead, A. 1954. *The Aims of Education.* New York: New American Library.

Notes on Authors

Bruce O. Barker is Department Chair, Media and Educational Technology at Western Illinois University. Address: College of Education and Human Services, Macomb, IL 61455.

Michael F. Beaudoin is Dean and Associate Professor of Education at the University of New England. Address: University of New England, College of Professional and Continuing Studies, 11 Hills Beach Road, Biddeford, ME 04005.

Tom Clark is a distance education consultant. Address: Tom Clark Consulting, Box 91, 1319 Carroll Avenue, Ames, IA 50010-0091.

Peter S. Cookson is Associate Professor of Education at The Pennsylvania State University. Address: The Pennsylvania State University, Adult Education Program, 403 South Allen Street, Suite 206, University Park, PA 16801-5202.

Patricia González is Adviser to the Administrative Secretary at the National Autonomous University of Mexico. Address: Margaritas #49, Colonia Florida, Mexico D. F. 01030, Mexico.

Charlotte N. Gunawardena is Assistant Professor at the University of New Mexico. Address: University of New Mexico, Training and Learning Technologies Program, College of Education, EOB 103, Albuquerque, NM 87131.

Christine S. Jones is Assistant to Director at the Center for Science, Mathematics and Technology Education at Colorado State University. Address: Colorado State University, Center for Science, Mathematics and Technology Education, B304 NESB, Fort Collins, CO 80523.

Marie A. Kascus is Librarian at the Central Connecticut State University. Address: Central Connecticut State University, 1615 Stanley Street, New Britain, CT 06050.

Greg Kearsley is Adjunct Professor in the Department of Educational Leadership at George Washington University. Address: George Washington University, 2134 G Street NW, Washington, DC 20052.

Farhad Saba is Professor at the San Diego State University. Address: San Diego State University, Department of Educational Technology, 5500 Campanile Drive, San Diego, CA 92182-1182.

Frank Tallman is Associate Professor of Education and Director of Educational Leadership at the University of Sarasota. Address: University of Sarasota, 5250 Seventh Street, Sarasota, FL 34235.

The American Journal of Distance Education

The American Journal of Distance Education is published by the American Center for the Study of Distance Education at The Pennsylvania State University. **The Journal** is designed for professional trainers; teachers in schools, colleges and universities; researchers; adult educators; and other specialists in education and communications. Created to disseminate information and act as a forum for criticism and debate about research in and the practice of distance education in the Americas, **The Journal** provides reports of new research, discussions of theory, and program developments in the field. **The Journal** is issued three times a year.

SELECTED CONTENTS

For information write to:
The American Journal of Distance Education
The Pennsylvania State University
110 Rackley Building
University Park, PA 16802-3202
Tel: (814) 863-3764   Fax: (814) 865-5878
Web: http://www.ed.psu.edu/ACSDE/

Date Due

ILL			
4175497			
4/19/04			